Praise for *Before You Quit*

This book will propel you to realign your perspective on what is important in your spiritual journey. This book messes with what we have always thought is important in our spiritual journey. Every chapter is thought provoking and challenges you to keep pushing forward for His glory.

BRUCE TERRY | Lead Pastor, Liberty Church, Birmingham, AL

Throughout life, I have found myself faced with circumstances greater than my ability to overcome. The overwhelming urge to quit is something I believe we have all faced, and will certainly face again. In Doug Gehman's book *Before You Quit*, he gives you key principles not only to help stand and endure, but for how to dig deep and fight for the greater vision and purpose of our lives. If you are in a season of struggle, or just can't seem to get rooted in your career, ministry, or community, this book is a must read! Let me encourage you, before you resign, throw in the towel, or turn and run away, read this book!

NATHAN POOLEY | Lead Pastor, Upper Room Church

You won't find the word *grit* in the Bible, but it's there nonetheless. Scripture is brimming with gritty examples of individuals full of persistence and courage to be the person God called them to be. I've had the distinct privilege in my life to be surrounded by courageous people, my dad and mom being at the forefront. This new book by my friend Doug is not only wonderfully written, but will challenge and encourage you to build up your courage and endurance to be all that God has planned for you to be.

ANDREW PALAU | Evangelist and author

Douglas Gehman knows what he writes about! I have a long-time friendship with him and have been privileged to serve as his pastor for several years. He has persevered through many times that others wouldn't have. His integrity is too rare in today's culture. He is a proven leader and communicator. I am SO grateful for this new addition to every resilient leader's library.

DOUG HOLMES | Senior Pastor, Christian Life Church, Milton, FL

In *Before You Quit*, my friend Doug Gehman has addressed, with real insight and inspiration, the challenge we all face, no matter the pursuit. I have gained renewed strength for my own journey by reading his book, and I am a convinced that you will as well!

JOSH LIPSCOMB | Lead Pastor of Liberty Church

Even if you're not on the verge of quitting something, life takes a toll on all of us . . . draining our perseverance level. Doug has written an essential book that refuels our tank to overflowing, helping us go the distance . . . with purpose and joy!

DAVID MAYO | General Manager, WHBR TV Christian Television Network Pensacola, FL

I was delighted to read the outstanding book *Before You Quit* by Doug Gehman. It is a book that is way past due for Corporate Executives, evangelical leaders, pastors, missionaries, and all who have a desire to fulfill their life's calling and purpose. In my 40+ years of ministry, I can think of many, many instances where this book could have circumvented many who quit before the fulfillment of their objectives. I will be making this a must read for members of our organization. Doug has made this a great read with many outstanding quotes and his own personal experiences to highlight each chapter and to drive home the theme of this book. You won't be disappointed, and you will be recom

DAVID KERR | Executive Director of the Globa

In a culture that seems confused, divided,
a reminder to build life on truth and to pe
challenge to finish well and finish strong! `
reminding us to not grow weary in doing we

D1372965

JOHN SPENCER | Senior Pastor at Coastline Calv

This is an essential book for our times. I have known Doug for over a decade and have learned that to know Doug is to know resilience. From the challenges of raising a young family on a shoestring as a missionary in Southeast Asia to leading a missions agency into the twenty-first century, to pressing forward when most his age are looking back, Doug continues to persevere. If you are thinking of quitting, read this book; it may just change your life.

MIKE DOYLE | Lead Pastor of Movement Church NYC

Augustine of Hippo wrote of perseverance as a separate gift of God's grace that empowered a believer to persist to the end. Doug Gehman reveals that character quality in his life from a perspective of God's grace, but also viewed from man's choices of faithfulness. *Before You Quit* is a balanced look at the tools our Father provides to encourage all believers to continue walking His path, in spite of the hardships.

ROBERT GRIFFITH | Dermatologist and certified in Myers-Briggs Type Indicator

I highly recommend to you my friend Doug Gehman's must-read new book *Before You Quit*. Many in our generation start out strong, but find themselves quitting during times of difficulty. This impactful book takes us on a journey of learning to find grace from our God that causes us to refuse to quit when facing challenging seasons in our lives. We can then experience the fulfillment of God's purposes as we live a life of perseverance that brings glory to Him.

LARRY KREIDER | International Director, DOVE Intl. and author of over 40 books

In the world of ministry, the most powerful enemy we have is discouragement. Discouragement sometimes causes us to walk too close to the edge of safety, it can cause us to feel hopeless, and it can push us to a place of no return. I know because I have walked there. Doug Gehman's new book *Before You Quit* is a powerful dose of uplifting reality, energetic encouragement that reminds us that no matter how hard the road may become, there is hope. It is filled with examples of others who have made it, scriptural edification, and personal stories from his own life that can be a lifeline to other leaders. This is not just "another book on a needed topic," it is a book from the heart of a leader who has been there.

JAMES G. GRAHAM | President, International Gospel Outreach and Founder/President, Access to Growth Life Coaching and Training

Doug Gehman has successfully articulated the most essential ingredient that every person must have for success—perseverance. His insights are both profound and practical. Doug is writing not from a mere theoretical perspective, but he has lived out his message in this book. You will enjoy the read and eternally benefit from the insights!

DANNY TICE | Lead Pastor, Bay Shore Community Church

I met Doug Gehman at a conference, but I got to know him on a visit to the mission field . . . where he was "getting it done." Our church worked with Doug for many years during the trying and dangerous days of the civil war in Sri Lanka. Doug's "against the odds" perseverance was the key that enabled him to plant church after church in the most difficult of times. If anyone knows about perseverance, it's Doug Gehman. Now turn the page and get ready to be inspired!

MICHAEL FLETCHER | Senior Pastor, Manna Church

Before You Quit is authentic advice stained with the sincerity, honesty, and conviction of a man who has tasted the price of perseverance. These words will inspire you to hold steady in your personal storm and give you the capacity to inspire others not to give up.

MICHAEL P. CAVANAUGH | President, Elim Bible Institute and College

Having been in ministry both as a missionary and a mission administrator for over forty years, I place *Before You Quit* at the top of the list of anyone considering serving in missions—in fact, for any Christian service. Sharing from his personal experiences, coupled with stories from history, and based upon biblical foundations, Doug has written a must read. This is a relevant and vital word for the church today written from a true friend who has and is persevering!

STEVE SHANK | Strategic Coach, Eastern Mennonite Missions

BEFORE YOU QUIT

Everyday Endurance, Moral Courage, and the Quest for Purpose

DOUG GEHMAN

MOODY PUBLISHERS

CHICAGO

Edited by Michelle Sincock
Interior Design: Ragont Design
Cover Design: Charles Brock
Cover illustration of ladder copyright © 2016 by jozefmicic / iStock (521619030). All rights reserved.

All websites and phone numbers listed herein are accurate at the time of publication, but may change in the future or cease to exist. The listing of website references and resources does not imply publisher endorsement of the site's entire contents. Groups and organizations are listed for informational purposes, and listing does not imply publisher endorsement of their activities.

Library of Congress Cataloging-in-Publication Data

Names: Gehman, Doug, author.
Title: Before you quit : everyday endurance, moral courage, and the quest
  for purpose / Doug Gehman.
Description: Chicago : Moody Publishers, 2020. | Includes bibliographical
  references. | Summary: "How Non-Quitters Changed the World You're
  exhausted. As you see your time and joy being spent on something that
  isn't going the way you planned... some days you wonder if it'd just be
  better to quit. Whether it's now or later, we're all faced with a choice
  between good and easy, between continuing on through difficulty or
  giving up. When that day comes, what will you choose? Doug Gehman
  observed firsthand how God used one man's relentless perseverance to
  change a country, and it changed him. In this book he shares dozens of
  stories of ordinary people who did extraordinary things for the kingdom
  of God because they simply kept going-through pain, discouragement,
  loss, and failure. He'll teach you how to cultivate a gritty
  perseverance that counts the cost and follows through. Become a person
  of courage and commitment and it'll cost you dearly, but it will change
  your life forever"-- Provided by publisher.
Identifiers: LCCN 2019041456 (print) | LCCN 2019041457 (ebook) | ISBN
  9780802419415 | ISBN 9780802498007 (ebook)
Subjects: LCSH: Perseverance (Ethics) | Christian life.
Classification: LCC BV4647.P45 G44 2020 (print) | LCC BV4647.P45 (ebook)
  | DDC 248.4--dc23
LC record available at https://lccn.loc.gov/2019041456
LC ebook record available at https://lccn.loc.gov/2019041457

Originally delivered by fleets of horse-drawn wagons, the affordable paperbacks from D. L. Moody's publishing house resourced the church and served everyday people. Now, after more than 125 years of publishing and ministry, Moody Publishers' mission remains the same—even if our delivery systems have changed a bit. For more information on other books (and resources) created from a biblical perspective, go to: www.moodypublishers.com or write to:

Moody Publishers
820 N. LaSalle Boulevard
Chicago, IL 60610

1 3 5 7 9 10 8 6 4 2

Printed in the United States of America

For Ray

CONTENTS

Foreword 9

Introduction 13

1. The Battle for Perseverance 23

2. Difficulty Involves Loss 33

3. Everyday Endurance 55

4. Aspirations for Greatness 69

5. Greatness from God's Perspective 79

6. Moral Courage 93

7. Perseverance and God's Consummate Purposes 107

8. Self-Care: Thriving in Difficulty 121

9. Perseverance as a Lifestyle 143

Epilogue 157

Acknowledgments 165

Notes 169

FOREWORD

I deeply appreciate Doug Gehman for writing this very much-needed book on the power of perseverance. Too many people early in life hold a vision for something greater than themselves and then they flame out. You find people asking, "Whatever happened to Joe? He had such a promising future."

When I was a teenager and began taking the Word of God, the Bible, seriously, there was a verse that I really had trouble accepting. In John 14:12, Jesus declares, "Truly, truly, I say to you, whoever believes in me will also do the works that I do; and greater works than these will he do, because I am going to the Father."

I wrestled with that promise because I just couldn't believe what it said. Was I reading it correctly? Maybe the translation was off, so I checked other translations and commentaries. They all basically said the same thing.

Jesus actually said His faithful followers could do the great works He did because He was returning to His Father and leaving His Spirit to indwell us, and we had to have faith in Him and His promises.

Jesus calls us to an active, ongoing, persistent faith, a life-long commitment. We can do great things for Him when we continue to persistently believe in Him, trust Him, and obey.

God created us for greatness. He created us for something greater than ourselves. He created us to accomplish His purposes through us. When we make it our aim to see life from God's perspective, and trust and obey His principles, He can then use us to accomplish anything we plan for His glory.

Like me, evangelist Doug Gehman has seen too many people give up. They simply quit. Too many people who started out with vision and passion end up finishing their life with cynicism, boredom, or complacency. What happened? They lost the power of perseverance.

Doug rightly points his readers to a lifelong commitment to trust and obey the promises and principles of God, which lead to perseverance and finishing well. Jesus reminded His followers that following Him would not be easy. He actually said His followers would be hated and suffer on His account, but that if they were faithful and persevered until the end, they would receive the crown of life (Rev. 2:10).

Missionary William Carey is attributed to saying, "Expect great things from God; attempt great things for God." What a powerful creed! What ambition! But it requires faith and perseverance. Perseverance is foundational. You may have vision, dreams, and big ideas, but without faithful perseverance and a reliance on the indwelling Jesus Christ in your life you will flame out.

This book is a must-read if you are thinking about quitting. Doug invites his readers to carefully and prayerfully examine how endurance teaches us something powerful about the eternal grace and all-sufficiency of God. The one who endures will gain so much more than anything they ever lose on this earth.

Are you on the verge of giving up? Have you given up? Are

you in the second half of your life with nothing but regrets? It's not too late to rebound. Doug challenges us to see life and time from God's eternal perspective and to finish strong. Doug implores his readers to apply the reality of eternity to their daily pursuits, commitments, and attitudes. Living with heaven in view with an eternal perspective gives us vision, drive, and perseverance. What an exciting way to live!

Back in December of 2017, I was diagnosed with stage 4 lung cancer. I remember jokingly telling the oncologist, "What happened to stages 1, 2, and 3?" He then told me I had only four to nine months to live. Thank God, He extended my life, but I'm fully aware that by the time this book goes to press I may be in heaven.

During one of my visits with the oncologist following chemotherapy, he asked me if I had any concerns. I answered, "Just one. Will I see you in heaven?"

I'm eighty-four years old and dying from cancer, but I'm ready for heaven. I've preached on heaven my entire life. I've had the privilege as an ambassador for God to lead many to Jesus Christ and the absolute assurance that, when they die, they will spend eternity in heaven.

When the news got out that I had terminal cancer, I began receiving hundreds of letters and emails from people thanking me for introducing them to Jesus and preparing them for heaven rather than that other place that we seem not to want to mention anymore. How I wish they had written to me earlier.

Once people realized I only had a few months left on this earth, they began asking me, "Luis, what is the key to finishing well?"

My initial reaction was, "I don't know. I haven't finished yet." But upon hindsight I do believe finishing well and perseverance are the results of a life of daily renewal; spending time every day in prayer and meditation; delighting yourself in the Lord; trusting and obeying the promises of God; delighting yourself in fellowship with other believers by putting roots down in a local church; being willing to submit to wise, godly mentors; fulfilling your God-given dreams and passions; and winning souls.

Most people who don't finish well, who don't persevere, stopped experiencing daily inner renewal, union, and communion with God. They reached a point where perseverance was trying to do a lot of stuff for God in their own power rather than resting in the power of the indwelling resurrected Lord Jesus in their life (Gal. 2:20). They became "me-centered" rather than "God-centered."

If that is you, then *Before You Quit* is a must-read. Quitting is not an option. Don't give up. There is hope. You can finish well.

Doug shows how you can leave a legacy of faithful persistence through daily humility and patience in life's storms; through reliance on the indwelling Christ as you pursue your dreams and aspirations; and through moral courage to accept that life is not always easy, nor fair. But when you embrace God's all-sufficient grace, life can be extremely successful and rewarding.

So stand strong. Don't quit. Trust and obey. Finish well!

Luis Palau

INTRODUCTION

I remember when perseverance was first powerfully illustrated to me. It was 1981, and I was twenty-six years old. Our family was nearing the end of a three-year internship in Southeast Asia with an itinerant evangelist. I'll call him WC. My wife and I, our two young children, and a handful of Thai and Philippine team members had been helping WC pioneer an evangelistic outreach ministry in Thailand.

WC's vision was to preach the gospel to "tens of thousands of people." WC was not new to Asia. He and his wife and young daughter first went to Indonesia in 1968. For three years they lived in a village on a remote island of the vast Indonesian archipelago. Their second child, a daughter, was born there. She fell victim to infectious pneumonia, and because they were far from medical facilities, and could not reach help in time, she succumbed to the disease. Brokenhearted and grieving, the family returned to America to heal.

After a time of recovery, their home church sent them to India to work with an evangelist who for ten years had been preaching the gospel to millions of people. The year in India, where WC was given an opportunity to preach to multitudes, transformed his life and gave him a vision for Southeast Asia.

In 1977, WC settled his family into an apartment in Hong Kong and launched a new vision: to duplicate what he had experienced in India and preach the gospel to large crowds in Southeast Asia, beginning in Thailand. I joined him on his first trip in April 1978. WC picked me up at Hong Kong's International Airport, and a few days later he and I, and a third young man from North Carolina, flew to Thailand. When we arrived in Bangkok, WC shared his vision with a group of missionaries and Thai leaders. With one accord they discouraged him. "This is a Buddhist country," they said. "Large crowds will never attend a Christian meeting here."

WC stomped back to our hotel and vented to me about their lack of vision. "These people have no faith! Well, God is going to do something amazing in this country!" What WC lacked in tact, he made up for in dogged determination. What he lacked in resources, he made up for in belligerent faith and big prayers.

WC bought an old 1960s British-made white Ford van in Hong Kong for $600, and shipped it to Thailand. From the day it left the port, the van was in bad shape. We named it Lazarus because it died again and again, and we had to continually raise it from the dead. For three years, we drove that worn-out van all over Thailand, stuffing it with equipment, luggage, and people. We parked it in dusty fields and public parks, set up our meager stage, lights, and sound system, and preached the gospel to the Thai people. Along an endless road of forgotten little towns and villages, we repeated this routine over and over, proclaiming the stories of Jesus Christ to measly crowds, proving to everybody, naysayers and believers alike, that the faithless discouragers were right.

But WC would not quit. He kept plodding, often praying with weeping, asking God for Thailand's multitudes. He planned, he prepared, he pushed, he prayed, and he preached, expecting God to move in Thailand, always looking for it to happen at the next event. Under the gritty leadership of WC, we fasted and prayed and worked, believing God for the multitudes. And WC wore me out with his tenacity.

In the spring of 1981, as we neared the end of our internship, we drove Lazarus to the northern regions of Thailand near the infamous Golden Triangle[1] for one final outreach. Frankly, I was looking forward to finishing this internship. WC had been tough to work for. One more outreach, and we would return to the United States for furlough. When we arrived in the village of Thoeng, WC grumbled to me, "Why did we agree to a ten-day meeting here? If I had known how small this place was, we would have planned for only three or four days!"

Resigned to yet another dismal meeting, desperately short on finances, but determined to go forward in faith, we set up camp in an abandoned schoolhouse on the back side of an old soccer field. The school was a dilapidated three-room wooden structure built in the traditional Thai style, on stilts four feet off the ground. There was no electricity. We had to run a line from a kindly neighbor's house to provide one light bulb to each of the school's three rooms that became our hotel. There were no toilets or places to bathe. We built bamboo shelters for each. Years before, rats had claimed the school as their home. Every night, when our family rolled our mats out on the rough wooden floor, we could see rats running along the dusty rafters above our heads. My wife refused to let me turn off the light bulb at night for fear the rats might come down and bite our children while we slept.

As we had done innumerable times before, we built a simple stage at one end of the soccer field and set up our simple lights and sound system and arranged for electricity from the kindly neighbor. Our Thai team fanned out through the area distributing handbills and announcing over loudspeakers about a "Free Good News Meeting." On the first night, about three hundred people showed up, a big surprise. On the second night, six hundred came. Then twelve hundred. Then twenty-five hundred. Each night, the crowds kept growing. Somewhere around the fourth or fifth day, trucks full of people began arriving midafternoon. We had no idea who hired the trucks. They arrived, dropped off their load of people, and left to pick up more. Scores of people of all ages clamored off the trucks and found spots in the grass near the stage. They sat down and covered their heads with newspaper to protect themselves from the hot, tropical sun, and waited for three hours!

When the meeting started, our Thai team sang songs of praise to the Son of God as they had done innumerable times before, and then we preached the gospel from the Bible about this amazing person named Jesus Christ whom God had sent to the world in love. After the meeting each night, many refused to leave. Hundreds set up camp on the field. Some sought shelter under the schoolhouse directly underneath us. Others tried to join us in our rat-infested classroom, but our Thai colleagues mercifully shooed them away.

By the ninth night, twenty thousand people poured onto the soccer field to hear the gospel. It took them hours to arrive, walking, riding on bicycles, and in nearly one hundred trucks and other vehicles that parked nearby. Except for the modern transportation that brought people, the crowds made us feel like we were reliving the Gospels where Jesus ministered to the multitudes that came to Him.

WC and I preached the good news of Jesus Christ to a very enthusiastic multitude. We told stories about Jesus Christ: the woman at the well, blind Bartimaeus, the woman with the issue of blood, Lazarus, and many more. We prayed for the sick, and God healed some of them. We told the story of the cross and declared that Jesus Christ, God's only Son whom God had sent to us because of His great love for the world, gave His life for our sins, and then, after three days in the grave, He was raised from the dead by the power of God. "He is a Living Savior!" we said. "And because He is alive, because He is risen from the dead, He can do for you what He did for others in the Bible." Thousands eagerly prayed to Jesus and gave their lives to Him.

On the tenth and final night, the local police withdrew our permit to preach. Too many upset people in the area, they said. Still, nearly sixteen thousand people arrived at the field. WC announced we could not continue but offered to pray for everyone who needed prayer. While I stood by and watched in awe, thousands lined up to receive a simple prayer from WC. He spent hours, sitting on a wiggly old chair on that decrepit stage, praying for his beloved Thai people, one person at a time. In the years following the Thoeng event, WC preached the gospel to large crowds all over Thailand.

Why did the Thoeng event happen?

Whenever we reflect on a move of God and consider how

God shows Himself to people, we rightfully give God all the glory He deserves. This is His work! He deserves all the praise! But in every divine visitation, there is a human element. Somebody obeyed God and became the servant He used to carry His message.

For this moment in Thailand, WC was God's instrument and servant. And the key to this impact was WC's obedience and his willingness to persevere, his refusal to quit. God gave WC a vision to preach the gospel to multitudes. WC took ownership of that vision and would not allow anyone or anything to steal it from him. Against all odds, he pressed on, prayed more, labored through, and would not relinquish his vision for multitudes to hear the gospel of Jesus Christ. WC doggedly believed God for the impossible. And God honored his faith.

If WC had allowed the difficulties, the naysayers, the small crowds, the insufficient resources, the delays, and the disappointments to stop him, he would never have arrived at God's appointed moment in a little village call Thoeng. We can all learn from the examples of people like WC. God is looking for those who will "through faith and patience inherit the promises" (Heb. 6:12).

WHY DO PEOPLE PERSEVERE?

What drives such perseverance? What makes people put up with difficulties, delays, and struggles? The answer to that question is the big idea of this book. In short, it is because God gave them a vision for something, and they were willing to work, and wait, and push, and wait, and sweat, and suffer, and struggle, and wait some more . . . and *never quit* until the vision God gave them became a reality. British schoolteacher and shoemaker William Carey famously said, "I can plod."[2] Carey's vision to take the gospel of Jesus Christ to India in the late 1700s ultimately required a lifetime of faithful service and struggle to be fulfilled, but in the end, he proved that patience, tenacity, and a refusal to quit a God-given vision will pay off. He accomplished historic things in the founding of Christianity among the people of India. He is now honored as "the father of modern missions." His story continues to inspire people today to a life of service.

In this book, we will look at three kinds of perseverance: Everyday Endurance, Aspirations for Greatness, and Moral Courage. The three kinds of perseverance can be very different from each other. Sometimes they are interrelated.

Everyday Endurance is the response to difficulties that we all face in our day-to-day lives. Lines at the supermarket, traffic jams, delayed flights, broken-down automobiles, and rained-out birthday parties are a frustrating part of normal life for everyone. How we respond to such things is, in part, a litmus test of our ability to handle greater levels of difficulty. It can also reveal where our heart is in terms of demanding our own way or surrendering to Jesus and allowing Him to truly be the Lord of our life. In everyday endurance, sometimes we must push, and at other times, we must be patient. Humility and clarity about God's purposes help us to grow in wisdom to learn the difference.

Aspirations for Greatness are voluntary pursuits that involve difficulty. We engage these quests because of a hoped-for end. Sometimes that quest is personal, sometimes it is altruistic. For Christians, aspirations for greatness should be motivated by God's calling on our lives and our desire to accomplish great things for His glory. When we aspire to greatness, we pursue a goal that is greater than ourselves—at least the self that we currently are. Whether it is a physical, mental, intellectual, spiritual, philanthropic, financial, or creative goal, the aspiration to be or do something great requires us to focus, to work, and persevere. Author and psychologist Angela Duckworth says this kind of perseverance is called *grit*.[3] WC had a lot of grit.

Moral Courage is something else entirely. It is almost always involuntary. Even when God asks us to do something that requires great moral courage, like when God told Noah to build an ark for the saving of the world, what is asked is so difficult that it seems involuntary. Our response is to have courage, to be strong, to faithfully obey. Moral courage requires us to accept unwanted circumstances and walk through them to an uncertain end. It is bravely facing unwanted difficulty, enduring persecution or personal grief or life-threatening circumstances. It is the most difficult kind of endurance because the challenge may seem to have no foreseeable outcome, or offer no clear purpose. For those who embrace such challenges, and keep their faith in God, this kind of perseverance is also the most noble. Why? Because there is no guarantee that life will improve or even continue after I have endured. The only guarantee is that, in our perseverance, God will be glorified and we will become more like Christ (see Rom. 5:1–5)!

Oh, that more of us would have courage when we face difficult or even impossible challenges! At some time in our lives, all of us will be called upon to be courageous in difficulty. Whether those circumstances require us to persevere with quiet patience or bold determination, we will be called upon to trust God and to grow in our ability to endure. To allow Him to work in our lives in and through tough times. Oh, that more of us would have such courage in daily life, to aspire to be a person of great faith, and to accomplish great things for God, especially that He will be glorified by our obedience!

All of us can grow in our determination to keep a commitment we have made, to complete a task that is set before us, and to stick to a vision God has assigned to us. God wants to so saturate our souls with vision, and so infuse us with determination for what could be, that we will dream the impossible, reach for the unreachable, and refuse to quit no matter what obstacles are thrown in our way or how long the battle rages. God wants to give us the grit to endure every challenge we face until that day when His purposes are made complete in and through us.

God calls His people to great things, to noble endeavors with eternal value! But such transcendent ideals will never be realized without a struggle. I hope this book helps you focus on the noble goals to which you are called, to endure difficulty that will shape your life, glorify God, and perhaps change the world.

1

THE BATTLE FOR PERSEVERANCE

"Why all this weeping?
You are breaking my heart!
I am ready not only to be jailed at Jerusalem
but even to die for the sake of the Lord Jesus."

—The Apostle Paul (Acts 21:13 nlt)

Charles Frederick Peace was a burglar and murderer in England in the 1800s. He was finally caught in Blackheath and taken into custody. He was tried at Leeds Assizes, found guilty, and sentenced to be hanged at Armley Prison.[1] English evangelist Leonard Ravenhill describes that day:

> On the morning of his execution, Peace. . . . was escorted on the death-walk by the prison chaplain, who was reading aloud from *The Consolations of Religion* about the fires of hell. Peace burst out "Sir, if I believed what you and the church of God say that you believe, even

23

if England were covered with broken glass from coast to coast, I would walk over it, if need be, on hands and knees and think it worth while living, just to save one soul from an eternal hell like that!"[2]

Both Jesus and the apostle Paul expressed similar determination. "From that time Jesus began to show his disciples that *he must go to Jerusalem and suffer many things from the elders and chief priests and scribes, and be killed*, and on the third day be raised" (Matt. 16:21). Agabus the prophet warned Paul that if he went to Jerusalem, he would be "bound by the Jewish leaders . . . and turned over to the Gentiles" (Acts 21:11 NLT). Paul's friends begged him to cancel the trip. But Paul replied, "Why all this weeping? You are breaking my heart! *I am ready not only to be jailed at Jerusalem but even to die for the sake of the Lord Jesus*" (Acts 21:13 NLT).

Jesus, Paul, and even Charles Frederick Peace can teach us something about determination and perseverance. Perhaps the real reason Jesus and Paul persevered through difficulty is they saw something about God's purposes, which lifted them above an ordinary, temporal existence where the vision became more important than anything else, including personal safety. Perhaps we too—when we see something bigger than ourselves, when God touches our lives with His glory—will do something radical for Him at great personal risk. But without such a vision for God's purposes in and through us, without a transcendent experience with God that transforms our paradigm, determination and perseverance are simply much less likely.

It could be asked, "Do I need a transcendent experience

to have perseverance?" Is not the human will enough? Do not human beings have within themselves the drive to live, survive, achieve, to be great, and stand for honor and courage? Do we really need outside impetus? These are legitimate questions. The apostle Paul recognized the human propensity for courage and even ultimate sacrifice. "Very rarely will anyone die for a righteous person, though for a good person someone might possibly dare to die" (Rom. 5:7 NIV). Humanity's ability to strive for something beyond themselves is a God-given quality, tainted now by sin, but still latent within us whether we acknowledge God or not. However, to strive for something selflessly, solely for the benefit of others, even for people who might be unworthy of our sacrifice, is something else entirely. Without a transcendent experience where God transforms the human heart—salvation by God's grace—such altruism is a rare thing. We are all too naturally self-absorbed. Selflessness is a characteristic unique to God. "But God demonstrates his own love for us in this: While we were still sinners, Christ died for us" (Rom. 5:8 NIV).

THE TROUBLE WITH TROUBLE

Every difficulty reveals *how badly we want something* and *how much we believe in something*. When difficulty confronts us, we have two choices: forsake the vision or fight well until the goal is reached. To quit is to abandon the hoped-for future. To persevere is to embrace pain, look disappointment in the face, and press courageously forward until the storm passes and the sun comes out again. But one thing is always true about difficulty: it reveals what we really believe and what we really want. Nobody ever ascended Mount Everest who didn't want to climb to the top. Nobody ran 26.2 miles who didn't want to finish a marathon. Nobody ever built a successful business who didn't want prosperity, and no one has ever conquered alcoholism who didn't want to be sober.

Do I quit and flee, or do I persevere to victory? These are the two options of *every* difficulty. The challenge will be tough, yet it is in the difficulty we discover what we really want, what we really believe, and where our motives really are. *Do I really trust God? Do I truly want this? Am I willing to press through?* At that moment, we decide what to fight for and what kind of person to be.

The great tragedy of our day is the fact that a great good— the life of ease, comfort, and safety with which we have become so accustomed—has stolen from us familiarity with difficulty. We simply do not know how to handle disappointment and pain, and therefore struggle when it comes near. Even Christians, who rely on God's sovereignty and acknowledge man's sinfulness, are influenced by our culture's self-assurance. We expect things to go well for us, and we place an inordinate amount of confidence in science, technology, and human wisdom to solve humanity's problems. Prosperity and a relatively long season of global peace has numbed us to the facts of history: humanity is not yet redeemed; we are still very broken and haven't changed as much as we think. Without God's transcendent work in our lives, we find it almost impossible to persevere through loss that does not have an obvious benefit to us. Tim Keller observes:

Sociologists and anthropologists have analyzed and compared the various ways that cultures train its members for grief, pain, and loss. And when all this comparison is done, it is often noted that our own contemporary secular Western culture is one of the weakest and worst in history at doing so.[3]

When trouble comes to us, it arrives as an unwelcome imposition and lays pain and uncertainty at our feet. We question and sometimes even blame God. Difficulty upsets our equilibrium. The pain of the loss is bad enough, but delays, insufficiencies, and worry about the future can be just as difficult. Difficulty robs us of or denies us access to something we value, and we either flee the circumstances or fight to endure.

QUIT OR ENDURE

When pilots are training to fly, they are taught to anticipate emergencies. In addition to mastering a specific airplane's flight controls and aerodynamic limits, they learn how to control their emotional responses under pressure. Pilots overcome reactive emotions such as denial, overconfidence, resignation, and panic by countering them with memorized response statements. For example, the corrective response for resignation is, "Not everything is hopeless. I still have choices." In every scenario, a pilot learns to *fly the airplane*!

I had a frightful experience with panic when I ran my first triathlon. Veteran triathletes warned me: "You survive the swim, kill the bike ride, and cruise the run." I trained for months, especially the swimming. I had a deathly fear of drowning from fatigue while swimming in deep water. To counter that fear, I trained in shallow water until I built up my confidence. On event day, I stood in line on a long pier for my turn to jump into the bay. At the horn, I leapt into the brisk water and started swimming. Before I covered a third of the distance, I was in trouble. Gasping for breath, my body quivering, and panic rising, I knew I was going to drown. A small lifeboat was floating nearby, only ten feet away. I desperately wanted to paddle over and grab for safety. Do I give up and escape the danger? Or do I stay the course and risk drowning?

As I floundered in the water, I gathered my wits and began telling myself, "I'm NOT going to drown! I've trained for this! I still have choices!" I pushed the panic down, steadied my breathing, and relaxed into the breaststroke until I got my wind back. Then, I pressed forward toward the shoreline. In short, I survived the swim! Then killed the bike ride, cruised the run, and came in fourth in my class!

After forty years in leadership, I've seen this kind of reactive behavior over and over. When people are confronted with difficulty, they quit "flying the airplane." Too many people squander great opportunity because they can't make it through the first test. We might make big sacrifices for the *idea* of a goal: we spend money, deny comfort, and even leave a stable life to pursue a dream. But then, when hardships come lurking from the shadows, and things don't go the way we hoped, the dream gets foggy, excitement wanes, and we are left with a simple choice: Do I quit or endure?

REALIZATION OF VISION

In his book *Nothing Like It in the World,* Stephen Ambrose writes about the building of the transcontinental railroad in America. It was a monumentally ambitious vision, the linking of the nation's two coasts by rail. In 1863, at the beginning of the project, some California enthusiasts decided to sponsor a launch ceremony. They invited a large selection of West Coast dignitaries to attend. Collis Huntington, one of the most important backers, was invited but declined, saying, "If you want to [celebrate] over the driving of the first spike, go ahead and do it. I don't. . . . Anybody can drive the first spike, but there are months of labor and unrest between the first and the last spike."[4]

We may have a vision to accomplish something, but that is only the beginning. The substance has not yet been realized. Vision will always be tested on its way to realization. Difficulty is the perfect test! It is God's way of hauling our values out of the shadows into the light. Whether it is a failed life goal or a personal tragedy, difficulty reveals what we really care about, how deeply rooted our faith really is, and how centered we are on accomplishing something God gave us to do in His purposes for our life. Difficulty refines our trust in God and proves our commitment to the task. The power of difficulty is found in the opportunity it gives us to practice determination and learn perseverance.

We must never forget that the *attainment* of goals (even God-inspired ones), the length of time it takes to get there, and the avoidance of difficulty along the way is never guaranteed.

Achievement of goals and victory over challenges are not endowments. They are won in the crucible of real-world pain and gritty courage, one intentional step after another. The Bible repeatedly reminds us of this great confluence of dreams and challenges in the journey toward the fulfillment of God's purposes.[5] Moses lived in obscurity for decades, and then struggled to lead the emerging Jewish nation for decades more before God's promises to him were fulfilled. Ironically, Moses did not live to see its full realization. Joseph was a privileged teenager when his jealous brothers sold him into slavery. His youthful dream of headship in his family was tested through years of unjust hardship in slavery and prison. It was finally fulfilled when he was thirty years old in ways that surpassed everyone's expectations.

How do I distinguish between my goals and God's? The simplest answer is found in a statement made by David in the Psalms. "I delight to do your will, O my God" (Ps. 40:8). When we settle this question about our motivations and make our primary goal in life to follow God's leading, to allow Him to be first in all things and His will to be our delight and passionate pursuit, then we position ourselves to discover a profound freedom. We can hear from Him and more confidently walk forward into dreams and goals that He gives us.

In another psalm, David states, "Delight yourself in the LORD, and He will give you the desires of your heart" (Ps. 37:4). As a young man, I took great encouragement from this psalm, believing that as I let God be first in my life, holding nothing back, but rather delighting in His will, He would shape my desires. I found that God directed my steps in my relationships, in career and job decisions, and even in things as mundane as term papers I had to write. I also discovered, as I learned to delight in the Lord, that I did not always pursue God with complete wholeheartedness and purity. I struggled against my fallen nature and its appetites. I fought depression and discouragement and struggled with self-confidence. But I kept my accounts short with God, by prayer, confession, and rededication to Jesus as my Lord. This is the story of every follower of Jesus—daily going forward in faith and continual realignment with Him and His purposes.

Somewhere between our hopes for a trouble-free life and the reality of difficulties, we *can* experience God's grace *and* forward movement toward His designed goals. The key is in perseverance. Perseverance navigates through the sometimes shadowy and painful gap between unrealized goals and their ultimate fulfillment. The lessons we learn in the gap, on a patient but determined journey, teach us valuable perspectives about the God we serve and His amazing redemptive purposes for the world.

In the gap—whether that time is spent in passive, prayerful waiting like Paul in prison or in active service doing something that is less than we want out of life—God is testing us. Do I really value His ways? Do I trust His sovereignty? Am I willing to wait on His timing and conduct myself as a Christ follower in the interim? Am I willing to learn and grow in Christ through difficulty and delay?

Endurance teaches us about God's eternal grace at work within us to make us more like Jesus. When we see Jesus in our troubles, we can glory in them as a gift from God who allows us to share in His redemptive work on a broken planet. Endurance teaches us about the reality of a world broken by sin and what it cost God to bring salvation. While Christ's work is complete, there is a battle to be engaged and resistance to be overcome as we walk out our salvation and bring His gospel to the world. Determination, balanced with patience and humble surrender to God, is necessary. This is the story of Jesus' example. It is the story of the early church. It is our story. But God gave a promise to people who endure in their faith: "The one who endures to the end will be saved" (Matt. 24:13).

When delays, difficulties, and disappointments happen to us—whether we suffer from a tragic loss, an unexpected setback, or a self-inflicted wound by a bad decision—we lose something, and that loss presents us with a "quit or endure" challenge. Most loss fits into four categories: **time**, **fun**, **treasure**, and **relationships**, which we will explore in the next chapter and consider how we can endure, survive, and even thrive through loss to discover what God offers us in exchange.

Discussion Questions

1. How do God's calling on your life and your own aspirations connect or conflict?
2. How do you persevere through difficulty? In what ways does difficulty threaten to rob you of confidence and resolve?
3. In what context have you been tempted to quit instead of endure? What did that look like?

2

DIFFICULTY INVOLVES LOSS

"A man once gave a great banquet and invited many. And at
the time for the banquet he sent his servant to say to those
who had been invited, 'Come, for everything is now ready.'
But they all alike began to make excuses."

—JESUS (Luke 14:16–20)

At the pinnacle of his career, with His popularity soaring off
the charts and religious critics screeching outrage, Jesus begins
His journey to Jerusalem, knowing betrayal and death awaited
Him there (see Luke 13:22; Matt. 16:21; 20:17–19). He turns to
the crowds and says:

"If anyone comes to me and does not hate his own father
and mother and wife and children and brothers and
sisters, yes, and even his own life, he cannot be my disciple. . . . *So therefore, any one of you who does not renounce
all that he has cannot be my disciple.*" (Luke 14:26, 33)

At this juncture, Jesus seems to change the rules and make impossible demands on His followers. So, you really want to follow Me? Are you willing to be scorned and have your family turn against you? Will you give up your rights and comfort? Will you suffer with Me? Are you willing to die? If you want to follow Me, count the cost, because from now on it's going to cost you everything!

There are times when Jesus allows us to follow Him casually. But then, a moment arrives when casual followership doesn't work anymore. We all think we are dedicated. But when God takes something we value, then we learn how dedicated we really are. In this chapter we will review four values—our **time**, **fun**, **treasure**, and **relationships**—that, when they are taken, reveal our true commitment.

TIME

Much of Western culture is conditioned for efficiency, and therefore, we hate delays and unexpected developments. Although Christians profess a connection to eternity, we are influenced by our cultural framework and its values, including the attachment to time. A little lost time is upsetting. When big chunks of it slip away, we can get downright angry. Eugene H. Peterson says that we now live under the "assumption that anything worthwhile can be acquired at once. We assume that if something can be done at all, it can be done quickly and efficiently."[1]

From a naturalist perspective, billions of years have passed since the "Big Bang" time/space singularity, an expanse that stands in ironic contrast to a single human life span. Even with modern advancements in medicine, an average American only gets about 78.8 years.[2] And so, the naturalist declares, "Live every moment to its fullest, because it is all you get!" This view stands in glaring contrast to the biblical perspective of time, without which, delays, difficulties, or tragedy can produce deep bitterness.

The Beginning of Digital Time

In 1934, American historian and sociologist Lewis Mumford pondered modern man's obsession with time and the technology that emerged to manage it.[3] He asked, "Where did the machine first take form in modern civilization?"[4] Ironically, Mumford observes, the clock was one of humankind's first modern inventions, developed to call Christians to prayer! Mumford asserts that the technology eventually "dissociated" time with the natural rhythms of life and bound us to the clock's "product": seconds and minutes.[5] Neil Postman is even more blunt:

> With the invention of the clock, *Eternity ceased to serve as the measure and focus of human efforts.* And thus, though few would have imagined the connection, the inexorable ticking of the clock may have had more to do with *the weakening of God's supremacy than all the treatises produced by the philosophers of the Enlightenment.*[6]

Are Mumford and Postman claiming that the clock killed God? Perhaps. At a minimum, they suggest our preoccupation with mechanical time diminished God in man's hearts. Astronomer Carl Sagan seems to bolster this view. In Stephen Hawking's *A Brief History of Time*, Sagan asserts, "This is a book about God . . . or perhaps about the absence of God."[7] Sagan suggests that, with what we now know about infinite time and space, there is no more reason for God, because there is nothing left for Him to do!

For Christians, there are important issues here—not with the clock itself, but how we relate to time and the values of our culture. I was recently sharing with a talented emerging leader who was training to assume leadership in a growing organization. About a year remained for the transition to take place, and he was impatient with the current senior executive. After listening for a while, I asked him, "Can I offer you a suggestion?" He responded with an eager yes. "Consider how you can make this final year the best it can be for your boss," I continued. "You have decades of leadership ahead of you, with lots of time to implement your ideas. For this coming short season, serve your boss. Make serving him your mission, nothing more. When the time comes for him to retire, he will gladly hand the reins to you, and will advocate your leadership to the rest of the team."

When we, as followers of Jesus, see time as a resource in God's control, we can steward time more patiently and view all our experiences, including the difficult ones, as opportunities to serve God and live for His glory. From a Christian, eternal perspective, the use of time is always a stewardship issue. In God's economy, faithfulness is measured primarily by how we treat people around us. Sitting at a long stoplight can be an opportunity to pray for a friend going through a hard time, or engaging in uplifting conversation with others in the car. How many opportunities have we wasted because, instead of engaging the people around us, we fume in a line, at a stoplight, or in an office and its clock?

Rather than viewing time as an infinite abstraction that proves God does not exist, Christians see Him in the realities of the cosmos: the passage of time through the rising and the setting of the sun as it rotates on its axis and the annual revolution of the earth around the sun. The passage of days and years remind us of God's magnificent, eternal glory, and of His wonderfully personal and present grace in our lives. He draws near to us in our experiences in the passage of time. He gave us connections with people, and the ability to share treasured moments and make memories along life's journey! For the Christian, modern technology has not robbed us of an awareness of God. Rather, it has enhanced our awe because we are reminded about how great God is, how small we all are, and yet how much He loves humanity. Even in our lost condition, God invaded the times of our lives in the person of Jesus Christ. Christians affirm what the Bible says: we live in the here and now, God came to us in the here and now, but life is eternal, and everything we do now is preparation for what will come in eternity.

> He has planted eternity in the human heart, but even so, people cannot see the whole scope of God's work from beginning to end. (Eccl. 3:11 NLT)

"And this is eternal life, that they know you, the only true God, and Jesus Christ whom you have sent." (John 17:3)

This is where the naturalist perspective is insufficient. If I view life only as a short earthbound existence that abruptly ends at the last beat of my heart, I will be not be able to have hope or patience in difficulty. But when I consider time from God's perspective, I understand that the brevity of my life and the vast eternal reality of God's are not disparate realities.

When I look at the night sky and see the work of your
> fingers—
> the moon and the stars you set in place—
what are mere mortals that you should think about them,
> human beings that you should care for them?
Yet you made them only a little lower than God
and crowned them with glory and honor.
You gave them charge of everything you made,
putting all things under their authority. (Ps. 8:3–6 NLT)

Christians understand that human life is not a random biological existence, evolved from primordial goo, scratching out a pointless eighty-year existence that abruptly ends and is gone. For the Christian, life is transcendent, formed and given purpose by a benevolent Creator, an eternal, enduring existence that explodes with meaning, value, and possibilities. The life we experience now is not our only reality or our final destination. Earthly life and time are merely a staging ground for something better, like the dress rehearsal for a magnificent play that will open soon. When we view life—even difficulty—from this perspective, everything changes! But this perspective is not natural to us; we must grow into it. Lysa Terkeurst says,

> Humans are very attached to outcomes. We say we trust God but behind the scenes we work . . . trying to control our outcomes. We praise God when our normal looks like what we thought it would. We question God when it doesn't.[8]

> To trust God is to trust His timing. To trust God is to trust His way. God loves me too much to answer my prayers at any other time than the right time and in any other way than the right way.[9]

The challenge for every follower of Jesus is to let eternity influence our everyday life, our outlook and pursuits, and our attitude toward difficulty. Simply put, living from an eternal perspective gives us the ability to thrive through every life experience, to be patient in traffic or with a difficult person at work, to endure disappointment or heartbreak, and even to *willingly* sacrifice for others by giving of our time, talents, and treasure in Christian service. Why? Because higher purposes are at stake. Our desire to be a witness for Christ—that our lives will reflect Him to our unsaved friends and family members—compels us to think about eternity and make the best use of the time we have. We want our example to draw people to Jesus. We want everything we do to confirm the claims of Christ. Our openness to God's work in our lives and our gratitude for what

Jesus did for us—making us more patient, more caring, more longsuffering in difficulty—motivates us to daily make choices that may have eternal consequences for people around us.

FUN

In the movie *Adrift*,[10] a true story about tragedy at sea, two newly acquainted friends, Tami and Richard, are chatting about Richard's experiences sailing alone on the open ocean.

"What's it like?" Tami asks.

"Miserable. Ugly awful," Richard replies. "You are either sunburnt, sleep deprived or seasick, usually all at once. And constantly hungry. Always wet. And after a few days there's the hallucinations."

Tami comments about Richard's "hallucinations," then asks, "If it isn't fun, why do you do it?"

Tami's question is a pithy commentary on contemporary Western culture. Some say this preoccupation with pleasure and fun is unique to postmodernism. Perhaps, but the indictment cannot be placed at the feet of one generation. Whatever values young people have adopted today, including fun and entertainment, they inherited from previous generations who led the way in throwing off moral and cultural restraints. Americans who came of age in the 1960s experienced an unprecedented era of cultural transformation. The marks of this shift—promiscuity, experimentation with mind-altering drugs, bold expressions in art, fashion, and music, and blatant challenges to established authority—emerged in the decade of the 1960s, but the seeds of revolution in culture and human behavior were planted long before.

The first half of the 1900s saw two world wars that killed more than one hundred million people. The time was one of the bloodiest centuries in human history.[11] The grief and loss that the United States—and much of the world—experienced during this time set the stage for the trauma of the 1960s. The 1962 Cuban Missile Crisis brought the United States and the Soviet Union to the brink of nuclear war.[12] Then, two prominent American leaders—President John F. Kennedy (1963) and civil rights leader Martin Luther King (1968)—were assassinated. And the controversial war in Vietnam that spanned nearly two decades (from the mid-1950s to the early 1970s) took the lives of sixty thousand young Americans.[13]

Millions of young people who were coming of age in this milieu gave up on a system they felt had betrayed them. Abandoning long-held traditions, they adopted devil-may-care lifestyles filled with drug use, sexual promiscuity, and open hostility to established authority. For the first time in history, a new media called television broadcast the images and social angst from coast to coast. Like tectonic plates, American culture shifted. By the early 1970s, the Vietnam War was over, and a sitting president (Richard M. Nixon) had resigned over further scandal. The die was cast, and subsequent generations became the inheritors of a new kind of hedonism that declared, "If it isn't fun, and if it doesn't make me happy, why would I do it?"

Years later, Neil Postman observed that television

advanced this new preoccupation with fun.[14] Television inadvertently usurped the historic place of printed news and mutated the public's hunger for information into a lust to be entertained:

> *Entertainment* is the supra-ideology of all discourse on television. No matter what is depicted ... *the overarching presumption is that it is there for our amusement and pleasure.* .... Everything about a news show tells us this—the good looks and amiability of the cast, their pleasant banter, the exciting music ... the vivid film footage, the attractive commercials—all these and more suggest that. ... A news show ... is a format for entertainment, not for education.[15]

God's View of Fun

But it is an incomplete framework to judge fun and pleasure by the capricious plumb line of modern culture. We need something more to get our bearings. God's Word provides a grounded perspective. God designed human enjoyment into the very fabric of creation. In the beginning, in the garden of Eden, God created a paradise made for humanity's well-being and pleasure. It was rich with life, diverse, safe, fulfilling, and complete in terms of humanity's every need. Unfortunately, sin ruined Eden for us, the result of which we became confused in our perceptions of who God is and what His intentions are for humankind. But God's purposes for humanity never changed. David Platt writes:

Our Creator has come to us to satisfy our desires in a way that nothing in this world can ever compare to. . . . Our taste buds are formed to find pleasure in good food. Our eyes are made to find pleasure in magnificent scenery. Our ears are fashioned to find pleasure in beautiful music. Our bodies are designed to find pleasure in physical intimacy with a spouse.[16]

Commenting about the tragedy of the lost condition of the world, C. S. Lewis says:

We are half-hearted creatures, fooling about with drink and sex and ambition when infinite joy is offered us, like an ignorant child who wants to go on making mud pies in a slum because he cannot imagine what is meant by the offer of a holiday at the sea. We are far too easily pleased.[17]

Without God, we grope for pleasure in temporal things that never satisfy. It's all just mud pies and slum living compared to the abundant life—of inner peace and contentment even in adversity—that God offers us. Christians know life can be rich with joy and meaning, but the joy originates from a transcendent source not bound to temporal pleasures. When we embrace this truth, we abandon shallow preoccupations and distractions to pursue joy and fulfillment in God and His ways. Christians do not seek to leave this world or merely wait for the rewards of eternity. Rather, in the midst of life's realities, including difficulty, we find refuge, solace, and courage in God's Word and His presence. By pursuing Him in prayer, worship, and connection with His people, we discover our greatest strength—Christ Himself! Genuine, sustainable joy is experienced in an obedient life dedicated to God's glory and purposes.

Christian joy, while *anchored in* eternity, is real now! "You make known to me the path of life; in your presence there is fullness of joy; at your right hand are pleasures forevermore" (Ps. 16:11). A God-centered person experiences joy in life's ups and downs. We "rejoice with those who rejoice" and "weep with those who weep" (Rom. 12:15). One of the attributes of Christian maturity is the discovery and the application of the truth that while not everything is fun, life can still be joyful. Mothers rise in the middle of the night to nurse a crying baby, denying themselves a good night's sleep, yet they find joy in caring for the needs of a precious child. Fathers climb out of a warm bed and go to work, even while suffering from a head cold and struggling in an unfulfilling job. They do this to provide for their family, and have joy in it, knowing their wife and children are nurtured by the stability they provide. Students press through classes and study and exams because they hold onto the hope of graduation and a career. Like the apostle Paul, who knew how to live with nothing and with everything, we too can find meaning and joy even when some things are difficult, even when not everything serves our preferences, and we can't see God's purposes in every detail (see Phil. 4:12–13 NLT). This is the stuff of spiritual maturity. This is the stuff of faith. This is what it means to persevere. Joyful hope and faithful living is God's foundational norm for His happy and grateful, yet brave and gritty people.

TREASURE

A rich, young ruler asked Jesus, "Teacher, what good deed must I do to have eternal life?" This man had everything one could hope to attain—success and affluence he achieved or inherited early in life—and yet he was troubled.[18] Jesus' response to him seems almost evasive: "If you would enter life, keep the commandments" (Matt. 19:17).

What is Jesus doing here? When I was in high school, I entered the science fair and spent weeks building a scale model volcano to illustrate one feature of earth's seismic activity. I proudly brought my chicken wire and Plaster-of-Paris model to the gymnasium, hoping to impress everyone with a fiery display of volcanic power. My assigned table, however, placed me next to a nerdy classmate and his mother-of-all-science-fair-projects—what looked like a fully operational Lunar Landing Module. Sigh. Comparisons can be brutal! Sometimes we just can't measure up. That's what Jesus is pointing out to the rich, young ruler. "You are not good enough, and you never will be, but go ahead and try. Here's God's list." The young man replied: "All these I have kept from my youth" (Mark 10:20). "What do I still lack?" (Matt. 19:20). Jesus doesn't argue. He just goes to the real issue:

> And Jesus, looking at him, loved him, and said to
> him, "You lack one thing: go, sell all that you have and
> give to the poor, and you will have treasure in heaven;
> and come, follow me." Disheartened by the saying, he

went away sorrowful, for he had great possessions. (Mark 10:21–22)

Jesus graciously sifts through the weeds of this young man's soul—pride, ambition, and naïve assumptions about human goodness and ability—and gets to the real issue: his treasure.

Professor and author Andrew Delbanco wrote the same thing more recently about Western culture: "We live in an age of unprecedented wealth, but in the realm of narrative and symbol, we are deprived. And so the ache for meaning goes unrelieved."[19] According to Delbanco, we have the riches, but no stories and no meaning to make it worthwhile. In this, Delbanco echoes Jesus: happiness and meaning do not come from riches and possessions. Wealth is nothing more than a fragile veneer over the real stuff of life, like watercolor paint on Easter eggs. It will never satisfy deeper human longings. The plea of a rich, young ruler—"What do I still lack?"—still echoes in the air of contemporary culture. The real stuff of life is found somewhere else.

A relationship with our Savior, Jesus Christ, provides the meaning we long for. Wealth may come to us and we are grateful for God's provision. But riches serve, not as an end in themselves, but as God's resource for our needs and as empowerment to serve others. Without this perspective, we are vulnerable to personal catastrophe when the resources we feel rightfully belong to us are taken away. Paul reminded Timothy of the trappings of such misplaced affections: "For the love of money is the root of all kinds of evil. And some people, craving money, have wandered from the true faith and pierced themselves with many sorrows" (1 Tim. 6:10 NLT).

When we discover the true wealth of knowing Jesus Christ, material losses we experience in life are less catastrophic. In fact, as we grow in Jesus we discover that giving is a joyful way to live. "God loves a cheerful giver," the apostle Paul declares to the Corinthians (2 Cor. 9:7). A friend of mine recently declared on social media, "Many years ago I said goodbye to the American dream, and picked up God's dream for my life. The reason why many don't step fully into what God has for them is because it takes extreme faith, trust, and obedience. Most Christians want to be in control of their lives. . . . When true Christianity is losing your life and finding it in Christ." Paul Maurer is a thirty-something single evangelist who travels the world preaching the gospel. He willingly gave up the pursuit of riches to pursue wealth of another kind: the riches of Christian service.

Another friend of mine, now in his sixties, has been a successful entrepreneur, owning and running many small businesses for most of his adult life. Bill is an ardent follower of Jesus. In recent years, he sold his businesses and went into full-time ministry, specifically to help men who struggle with addictions. He was recently offered a partnership in a new business venture but turned it down. He shared with me over breakfast, "I thanked the man for the offer, but told him, 'I have a much bigger venture that I'm working on right now: God's calling to help men.'" Bill gave up a lot of financial security to pursue a ministry calling, but like many of us who have made such decisions, he discovered that the riches of serving God are much more rewarding than material wealth. When we trade our earthly treasure for God's, we are never disappointed.

In fact, Christians are some of the most benevolent people on earth. Author Don Eberly says, "Religious giving accounts for a staggering sixty-two percent of all donations in the United States, according to the Center on Philanthropy at Indiana University."[20] Eberly said the same was true concerning charitable giving for victims of Hurricane Katrina that hit New Orleans in 2005:

> Victims of the hurricane gave dramatically higher marks to religious and charitable organizations such as the Salvation Army. . . . In a survey, residents gave churches the most favorable rating for their contribution to emergency relief, followed by nonprofits in general.[21]

Why is this true? Christians simply live and serve from their existential abundance! Love, kindness, mercy, and generosity flow out of what we have received in Jesus Christ. But let's face it. Kindness and generosity aren't always easy. We still think and act selfishly. We get tired of people asking for handouts. We deal with feelings of insecurity and need. People hurt us, and sometimes we encounter people who are seriously evil in their lusts for personal gain. But we can, by God's grace, exchange our love for earthly riches and store up treasure in heaven (see Matt. 6:14–21). When we have God's true riches, the gain or loss of temporal possessions is no real gain or loss at all. Why? Because we experience the glory of God and His rewards now even while we also wait for their complete fulfillment in an eternal home that awaits us in the future. In this life prior to heaven, there simply is nothing on earth—no amount of money or acclaim or worldly security—that surpasses the peace, joy, and sense of well-being that Christians experience in their relationship with Jesus Christ. As the apostle Paul said, God's peace "surpasses all understanding" (Phil. 4:7).

RELATIONSHIPS

My brother, Dale, committed suicide when he was twenty-seven years old. He had found Jesus a few years before and was following a call from God into music ministry. He served as a pianist and vocalist on his church's worship team, wrote worship music, and formed a Christian music group. But then, for reasons we still do not understand, he fell into a deep depression. Three months later, he ended his life. We were devastated. We came home from Thailand for the funeral to grieve with our family. After two months, we returned to Thailand, but I remember being overwhelmingly sad for a very long time. Now, decades later, I still ache when I think about Dale. I think about all that was stolen in his premature death: the creativity that was never realized, his many friends whose lives were thrown into turmoil, his future wife he would never meet, the children they would never have.

In tragedies like these, should we get angry and shake our fists at heaven, or should we embrace the terrible pain, allow God to comfort us, and let this overwhelming sorrow and grief shape us into the likeness of Jesus Christ? In Dale's death,

I learned the stark truth about Isaiah's words concerning the Messiah: He is "a man of sorrows and acquainted with grief" (Isa. 53:3). Jesus is touched with the feelings of our infirmities. This is the miracle and the beauty of the incarnation! He willingly entered this broken world; God became flesh and dwelt among us. When we talk about becoming like Jesus, sorrow and grief are a part of our journey because, like Him, we become willing to share in the sufferings of others.

In this tragedy, God allowed me to experience something that Jesus knows about this broken world and all that has been lost because of sin and human failure. What was even more profound was watching my parents walk honestly and bravely with God through the agonizing loss of a beloved son. Our family's tragedy gave us a personal glimpse into the loss God must continually experience when broken people make damaging choices. I look back on our experience now and see how, even in this tragedy, God was doing a redemptive work. He gave us a gift by teaching us how to have empathy. To come alongside someone in pain. To weep with those who weep. We had to walk through our grief, but now, even though the feelings of loss are still real, I can empathize with others who suffer the loss of a loved one.

As difficult as it is, pain is a part of the way we become like Christ. Pain and loss are realities in this broken world; Christian faith does not inoculate us from these experiences. In fact, our faith and our hope lead us to them and empower us to endure, overcome, and serve others in His name. These are Jesus qualities! When we embrace pain and loss, quitting or running from difficulty is never an option. Sometimes pain comes knocking at our door, and we must let it in. I look back now in wonder, with an ache in my heart for my brother, that God graciously allowed me to experience something of His amazing love for a broken world.

If you are a Christian, God has put His boundless love into your heart. When you suffer the loss of a relationship, either by death or separation, God can fill the void and enable you to grieve yet still have genuine hope in His goodness and promises. In this life, no human relationship is permanent, but God has promised us that He will never leave us or forsake us (Heb. 13:5). That reality makes it possible for you to truly love other human beings. He has placed His eternal nature—with all its power, perspective, values, and compassion—within your grasp. He enriched your life with the eternal quality of love, and while that love gives you joy and fullness, it also causes you to grieve when you suffer loss. But what makes our experiences different from the world's is this: we do not grieve like those who have no hope (1 Thess. 4:13).

WE ARE ETERNAL BEINGS

In the Christian faith, we do not run from suffering. Rather, we *embrace* it as the very heart and soul of our story. Christians know from the Bible, and we learn in personal experience, that nothing protects us completely from difficulty. But God empowers us to endure and overcome it. "In this world you will have trouble," Jesus said. "But take heart! I have overcome the world" (John 16:33 NIV). Suffering is rooted in human sin, starting when Adam and Eve turned away from God. Suffering, though, is the way God rescued us. Jesus surrendered the riches and security of heaven to confront the robbery and ravages of sin. He had to suffer to do this.

In like manner, we willingly suffer for Jesus. Though we have everything we need, we are willing to make sacrifices, knowing we are never poor. Though we are grafted into Christ's body, we are willing to be lonely, knowing we are never alone. Though we are safe, we willingly face danger, knowing death cannot hold us. Tim Keller says we should view losses as investments: "Weeping may last through the night, but joy comes with the morning. . . . Tears don't just give way to joy; tears produce joy! . . . The kind of joy you really need, is the product of tears."[22] Paul says, "For our present troubles are small and won't last very long. Yet they produce for us a glory that vastly outweighs them and will last forever!" (2 Cor. 4:17 NLT).

We will never be able to endure difficulty or overcome challenges if something on earth is more important to us than something in heaven, namely, Jesus. Yet when we release our grip on earthly values—time, fun, treasure, and relationships—to grasp what God offers us in His unfathomable forgiveness, His abiding presence, the promises of His Word, a purpose-filled life, and a secure future hope, something indescribable happens.

> But we *have this treasure* in jars of clay, to show that the surpassing power belongs to God and not to us. We are afflicted in every way, but not crushed; perplexed, but not driven to despair; persecuted, but not forsaken; struck down, but not destroyed. (2 Cor. 4:7–9)

We rightly cling to our temporal lives, and yet we cling even more determinedly to our eternal one. We don't yet perceive eternity in its fullness. As Paul wrote, "For now we see in a mirror dimly, but then face to face. Now I know in part; then I shall know fully, even as I have been fully known" (1 Cor. 13:12). But we perceive this eternal realm, we interact with it and the One who abides there, and through the Holy Spirit, God gives us His selfless agape love as a witness to its reality. That agape love—for Him and for others—"bears all things, believes all things, hopes all things, endures all things." That kind of love "never fails" (1 Cor. 13:8 NIV).

In ensuing chapters, we will explore Everyday Endurance, Aspirations for Greatness, and Moral Courage and discuss how, with foundations in a biblical and Christian worldview, we can grow in our ability to endure and overcome every difficulty for the glory of God.

Discussion Questions

1. What does Jesus mean when He says you must hate your family to follow Him?
2. How does time affect and perhaps challenge your faith in Christ?
3. In what way might fun or treasure distract your walk with God and be a detriment to your relationship with Jesus and God's calling?
4. What can you do to develop an eternal perspective?

3

EVERYDAY ENDURANCE

But I say, walk by the Spirit, and you will not gratify the desires of the flesh. For the desires of the flesh are against the Spirit, and the desires of the Spirit are against the flesh, for these are opposed to each other, to keep you from doing the things you want to do.

—PAUL (Galatians 5:16–17)

During the early years of our life in Asia, our family had to make visa runs from Thailand to Malaysia. On one excursion, because there were four of us (my wife, our two children, and me) and the trip was overnight, we booked a round-trip ticket by train in a private compartment. We spent a couple of days in Penang and then hopped on the train for the long haul back to Bangkok. When we stopped at the border, I joined the line at immigration. An attendant stopped me and said, "Just stay in your compartment. An official will come and stamp your passports." We waited an hour and then the train started rolling. Confused, I left our compartment to ask what was going on.

I found several immigration officers in the dining car drinking Thai coffee and smoking. I approached their table, showed my passports, and explained what happened. One of the officials examined my passports and replied, "You must get off this train at the next stop and return to the border!" Stiffening, I retorted, "We did what we were told! It's not my fault that no one came to our compartment! I have a wife and two children! I can't go back to the border!" Thrusting the passports at me, the official snapped, "That isn't my problem. There's nothing I can do. You must return to the border!"

I took a deep breath, changed my expression from mad dog to meek sheep, and said, "Sir, I am very sorry. I am new to your country, and I made a serious mistake. Can you help us?" The official's countenance changed immediately. He sat up in his chair and said, "Certainly! Give me your passports." I handed them back to him, he opened each one, stamped and signed them, and handed them back to me. I thanked him profusely and returned to my wife and kids. What just happened? A Proverb says, "A soft answer turns away wrath" (Prov. 15:1). I learned later that it is a serious breach of etiquette in Thai culture to embarrass people—especially persons in authority—by pointing out their failure. By my soft answer, I helped this Thai official "save face" in front of his colleagues. Whew!

It's always a breach of etiquette to be mean. Impatient behavior rarely produces anything positive. As followers of Jesus, we are expected to behave differently. As His witnesses, we represent Him. God asks us to make the needs of others more important than our own. That is the essence of Everyday

Endurance. We daily interact with individuals: a weary gate agent, a stressed restaurant server, or an overwhelmed single mother with three cranky children. They could be God's opportunities for us to offer a word of encouragement or a helping hand. Being Christlike by rising above our frustrations and giving assistance, we change the atmosphere. In a moment of crisis, a levelheaded person is probably the single most powerful human being in the world. Christians should lead the way in such situations!

Pastor and author Gordon MacDonald tells a story about being stranded in Hong Kong and meeting a fellow passenger who got a ticket. The man explained that he went to the counter and "used every bit of profanity I know . . . and demanded a seat on this next flight, and I got it." He suggested MacDonald do the same. MacDonald approached the agent, repeated the advice, and said, "Frankly, I'm not that kind of guy. . . . So, do you think you could help me out?" The agent said he'd try. MacDonald did not get a ticket. "The moral of the story," he reflected: "*Character doesn't always result in the kind of success one wants.* We don't develop character because it brings success; we develop it because it is . . . the God-pleasing way to live."[1]

IRRITATIONS AS OPPORTUNITIES TO PUT OTHERS FIRST

Perseverance is usually unpleasant! Comfort is gone and one is left with, well, discomfort and inconvenience. To persevere, we rise above inconvenience, embrace discomfort, and endure unpleasantness for a greater purpose.

Recently I was awaiting a flight from Chicago while a major summer storm hammered Atlanta. When we landed several hours behind schedule, the airport was in chaos. I spent the night in the terminal with masses of frustrated travelers. The saga reached its finale at 5:30 a.m. the next morning when my connecting flight was canceled. Wearily waiting in yet another line, sapped with fatigue, I rehearsed with clenched fists what I was going to say to the gate agent. But, as I stood there and fumed, I realized that whatever I did in the next few minutes would demoralize an already weary gate agent, and reflect badly on me and Jesus. I resolved to change my attitude. When my time came, I put on my nicest smile and said to the agent, "Good morning! Long night for you too?" She glanced at me suspiciously, and said, "Yeah . . . uh, how can I help you?" I explained my need, she found me a flight, I thanked her and left. It was all very brief and business-like. I'm sure she quickly forgot me. Better that than being remembered as the day's biggest jerk.

I replayed the story at a gathering of friends a few days later. A fellow business traveler commented, "Sounds like a rich man's inconveniences." What? Is that all the sympathy I get? Well, in truth, that's all the sympathy I should get. It's not like I was starving for food, dying of thirst, and exposed to the elements. I wasn't robbed or held at gunpoint. My house wasn't burned down, my wife wasn't attacked, and my children weren't kidnapped. I was simply inconvenienced. I lost a few hours' sleep in a climate-controlled airport terminal. Big deal!

We hate everyday difficulties! They strike at the heart of our sense of entitlement. We all tend to live in a box marked

"My Needs = Highest Priority." In that framework, instead of treating people like human beings, we treat them like objects in our way. To get out of the box, we must make the needs of other people more important than our own. That is not easy! We are inherently self-centered. Paul writes to the Romans quoting Psalm 14: "'No one is righteous—not even one! . . .' All have turned away; all have become useless. No one does good, not a single one" (Rom. 3:11–12 NLT).

Paul continues with comments about our mouths (an open grave), our tongues and lips (poison of snakes), and how much destruction is really in our hearts.[2] Ouch! In his letter to the Philippian church, Paul writes: "Let each of you look not only to his own interests, but also to the interests of others" (Phil. 2:4). Everyday difficulties vividly uncover our selfish inclinations. They also give us an opportunity to rise above selfishness and be a decent human being.

THE DARK SIDE OF PROSPERITY

A pastor friend of mine serves in New York City. When I was visiting recently, he told me about a big-box store in his Queens neighborhood. Living nearby are many recent-arrival immigrants. Every time the store restocks their shelves, the new immigrants virtually clean it out. They simply are not accustomed to abundance and assume the stock might be the last shipment ever! Those of us who are accustomed to the American lifestyle, on the other hand, take prosperity for granted. We live with abounding choices and distractions. Our culture of consumerism drums out an unrelenting demand for bigger, faster, better, cheaper. Stores respond, offering every imaginable product money can buy. Because we are used to speed and efficiency, we struggle to be nice when life goes sideways. But, there is a solution to this problem. It starts with accepting a simple reality: life randomly includes challenges and difficulties. C. S. Lewis wrote,

> The problem of reconciling human suffering with the existence of a God who loves, is only insoluble so long as we attach a trivial meaning to the word "love," and look on things as if man were the centre of them. Man is not the centre. God does not exist for the sake of man. Man does not exist for his own sake.[3]

As good as life is, and as much as we talk about God's love, when life doesn't reward us with what we want, or when things go bad and we suffer loss, our ability to reflect and express Christian love can erode with our circumstances. One of the biggest enemies to contentment and to our ability to endure disappointment is rooted in our expectations. When we believe "the grass is greener on the other side of the fence," when we obsess about our neighbor's house, or wardrobe, or vacations, or career, when we believe our life should be as good or better than what we perceive to be someone else's experience, we will be perpetually unhappy even when all our essential needs are met. The Bible calls this covetousness; it is clearly prohibited in the Ten Commandments (see Ex. 20:17), and its dangers are frequently repeated in the New Testament.[4] Contentment is never found in the accumulation of possessions, in human praise, or in beating out another person on the road to success. The apostle Paul was very specific about what contentment really is:

> But godliness with contentment is great gain, for we brought nothing into the world, and we cannot take anything out of the world. But if we have food and clothing, with these we will be content. But those who desire to be rich fall into temptation, into a snare, into many senseless and harmful desires that plunge people into ruin and destruction. (1 Tim. 6:6–9)

Accepting the fact that the accumulation of wealth or its loss is not the essence of happiness and fulfillment can temper our propensity to think we deserve more and better. Even the non-Christian world has discovered the incongruity of wealth and possessions as the definition of contentment. *Harvard Business Review* reported a study about consumer "stickiness." The study included surveys of more than seven thousand consumers and interviews with hundreds of marketing executives and other experts around the world:

> Our study bored in on what makes consumers "sticky"—that is, likely to follow through on an intended purchase, buy the product repeatedly, and recommend it to others. We looked at . . . more than 40 variables. . . . The single biggest driver of stickiness, by far, was "decision simplicity . . ." What consumers want from marketers is, simply, simplicity.[5]

The irony is, while abundance and convenience has improved our lives, we are not happier. The great paradox of our time is, we have everything we want and need at our fingertips, yet our stress levels are off the charts. In fact, psychologists have discovered that too many choices *increase* discontent. A study by psychologists Sheen Iyengar and Mark Lepper from Columbia and Stanford Universities—involving the sale of jams at a local food market—revealed that too many choices create not happiness but indecision![6]

Our family discovered this when we returned to live in the United States after fifteen years in Asia. We would sometimes go to the supermarket, not to shop, but to walk around and look at the massive varieties of food. We'd spend ten minutes—an eternity in grocery shopping time—in the cereal aisle, gazing at the overwhelming number of brands, flavors, grains, colors, and box sizes. In Asia, all we could find was corn flakes! How does anyone ever decide what to eat in this country! Iyengar and Lepper referenced research on this subject by psychologist Barry Schwartz: "Logic suggests that having options allows people to select precisely what makes them happiest. But as studies show, *abundant choice often makes for misery.*"[7]

Now, after having lived in the United States for nearly thirty years since our return, I can say that the more complex life we live here is not measurably happier than the simpler life we had in Asia. Life is more convenient, and we have more possessions, but in truth, we are more distracted. Unless we intentionally work at it, we struggle with being too busy, more discontented, and less connected with people. Possessions alone have little to offer in terms of human happiness and fulfillment. But in the sharing of our possessions and time with others—over a meal, in an outing to the beach, or in a community service project—we experience the real joys of life. True abundance, that which rises from our connection with Jesus and His overflowing presence in our lives, is most profoundly experienced in our relationships with other people and in Christian service. Happiness and contentment is found in shared experiences and memories we create in loving involvement with others. The apostle Paul was right! "Godliness with contentment is great gain" (1 Tim. 6:6).

THE JOY OF WORK AND REST

Life is almost always more satisfying when we slow down and simply enjoy the journey. The process of learning and contentment on the way to accomplishment enriches the soul. Developing personal interests for a future profession or a hobby, if pursued patiently and with a mindset to enjoy the journey, allows us to genuinely *enjoy* our work! In other words, perseverance can be rewarding when it is connected to an attitude of patient determination focused on learning and growing rather than simply producing an outcome. Mihaly Csikszentmihalyi studied people who worked for enjoyment without promise of money, fame, or the pressure of a deadline.

> Chess players, rock climbers, dancers, and composers devoted many hours a week to their [pastimes or hobbies]. Why were they doing it? It was clear from talking to them that what kept them motivated was the quality

of the experience they felt when they were involved with the activity. This feeling . . . often involved painful, risky, difficult activities that stretched the person's capacity and involved an element of novelty and discovery.[8]

Patience in work, and contented rest, have the same renewing qualities. When asked by his protégé John Ortberg what a person must do to stay spiritually healthy, Dallas Willard paused for a moment and then replied, "You must ruthlessly eliminate hurry from your life."[9]

In a recent survey by our church, 80 percent of responders indicated that stress, anxiety, and burnout were the big issues on people's minds. In a follow-up message, our pastor offered a simple Bible answer: "Take a Sabbath Rest!" Introduced on the seventh day of creation, the Sabbath pre-dates both Adam and Eve's fall into sin and the Law of Moses. "The Sabbath was made for man," Jesus later explained (Mark 2:27). God gave us a day every week for rest. The Sabbath is an amazing gift! What if we would apply the gift to our weekly routine? Not in a burdensome, legalistic way, but by an intentional decision to cease from all stressful activity for a few hours or an entire day. To divert from our normal schedule, and do something that is personally edifying or relationally nurturing might become one of our most revolutionary endeavors.

My wife has been an amazing asset to our marriage in this area. I tend to be a workaholic. She has helped me relax and enjoy the process of a project and not just worry over its completion. She has helped me build margins. She has helped me divert. She has helped me say "No." Listening to and learning from her gentle coaching has been one of the richest experiences in our marriage. Much of our inability to endure everyday challenges can be attributed to the chronic fatigue that builds up because we have not rested sufficiently and do not have margins in our lives, or because we have not learned how to enjoy the journey of life with its unpredictable rhythms instead of being obsessed with arriving at a destination. Maybe daily difficulties are God's reminders to slow down, enjoy the journey, take a rest, change our attitude, adjust our expectations, and rediscover our joy in Him.

LIVING THE GOOD NEWS

The power of the Christian faith rises and falls on how we handle difficulty and how we reflect Jesus by being kind or helpful to others. By slowing down, getting rest, and adjusting our expectations, we develop the reserves we need to handle life's annoyances and respond to challenges in a Christ-honoring way.

The little difficulties of life can be God's reminders. Difficulties are really opportunities to become more like Jesus and to better reflect His character along life's bumpy journey. At the beginning of this chapter, I referenced a few words from Paul's letter to the Galatians. He makes a profound comparison between "walking by the Spirit" and "gratifying the desires of the flesh" (Gal. 5:16), two postures that in Paul's words "are opposed to each other, to keep you from doing the things you want to do" (v. 17).

Paul first delineates the "works of the flesh" (vv. 19–21),

offering an unflattering list of bad behaviors, from drunken-ness and orgies to strife, jealousy, anger, and rivalries. How many of these have we allowed to influence our attitudes and behavior? Paul then offers an alternative list that he calls the "fruit of the Spirit," which is comprised of love, joy, peace, pa-tience, kindness, goodness, faithfulness, gentleness, and self-control. Paul reminds his readers that "there is no law against such things!" (vv. 22–23). In other words, you will not get into trouble—either by inner stress or outer conflict—when you live by the fruit of the Spirit! The key to living this way and avoiding the desires of the flesh is a simple matter of surren-der. When we die to ourselves and allow Jesus Christ to live in and through us, He produces the Holy Spirit's fruit in us. One could say it is almost automatic. A healthy tree produces good fruit. Our job is simply to surrender to the presence of Jesus in our lives and stay connected to Him.

> "Abide in me, and I in you. As the branch cannot bear fruit by itself, unless it abides in the vine, neither can you, unless you abide in me. I am the vine; you are the branches. Whoever abides in me and I in him, he it is that bears much fruit, for apart from me you can do nothing." (John 15:4–5)

We cannot live the Christian life on our own! The Chris-tian life is Christ in us, living through us. This is the most profound truth you will ever discover as a follower of Jesus. Whatever your weakness, whatever your vulnerability, you can overcome by simple surrender to Jesus in His death and in acceptance of His resurrection power in your life: "And those who belong to Christ Jesus have crucified the flesh with its passions and desires. If we live by the Spirit, let us also keep in step with the Spirit" (Gal. 5:24–25).

By leaning on Jesus and walking in His Spirit, you can grow through a difficult experience, including an unrewarding job, an unreasonable boss, or a difficult relationship. Unruly neighbors, distracted drivers, sick children, angry classmates, or an inattentive spouse give us opportunities to grow in our dependency on Jesus Christ for inner peace and godly behavior while we seek God for solutions to our troubles. We can learn to lean into Him. To endure with grace. To be patient and find words of kindness. To put strife, anger, jealousy, and impurity to death. And when the truth must be spoken, to speak it in love, which according to Paul is the most important thing we can ever do (see 1 Cor. 13; Eph. 4:14–15). The world needs more people with these qualities. Who better than the followers of Jesus to lead the way?

Discussion Questions

1. How is Everyday Endurance an opportunity to grow in Christlikeness?
2. How do you balance determination with patience?
3. When it comes to Everyday Endurance, what is the most difficult thing for you?
4. How can you work on persevering well so your witness for Christ is not damaged?

4

ASPIRATIONS FOR GREATNESS

For you formed my inward parts;
you knitted me together in my mother's womb.
I praise you, for I am fearfully and wonderfully made. . . .
My frame was not hidden from you, when I was being made
in secret, intricately woven in the depths of the earth.

PSALM 139:13–15

Running marathons has become a veritable American pastime. I've done three in my lifetime. As one multiple-marathoner kindly warned me when I was training for my first: "There is no way to complete a marathon without pain. Pain is the nature of marathons." Another helpful friend advised me, "Somewhere around mile eighteen you will hit a wall. You just have to push through it and get to the end."

An "Ironman" triathlon is even more difficult. There are Ironman triathlons all over, but the ultimate one is the original: the Ironman World Championship, popularly known as the Kona Ironman. The by-invitation-only Kona Ironman starts with a 2.4-mile swim in Hawaii's Big Island Kailua-Kona Bay, followed by a 112-mile bike ride through the Hawaiian lava desert, and finishes with a 26.2-mile run along the Big Island's coastline. Every year, nearly 2,500 people are invited to pay for the privilege to join a cohort of fellow fanatics in the ultimate suffer-fest for eight to seventeen hours. Their single aspiration? To conquer the ultimate race. Of those who start the race, many quit before the finish line, overwhelmed by injury or fatigue.[1]

GREAT EFFORT PRODUCES GREAT ACHIEVEMENT

Many people are driven to make money, acquire fame, or achieve something great. The ambition drives them to work hard, suffer through difficulties, and stretch themselves in the development of skills, expertise, or a competitive edge that they hope will bring huge rewards. Some aspire to influence or success in the private sector through business. Others want to succeed in public service. Often these aspirations are noble, to make a difference in society by bringing changes to public policy or government programs. In business, people have ambitions to introduce a new product or service that will improve the quality of life for many people. Sometimes, however, human aspirations are purely selfish, with motivations to attain wealth, fame, or power for its own sake regardless of its benefit to others.

On the other hand, many people are not enticed by the long slog to the top. They prefer an easier pace in life and a more casual rhythm. If we are in this group, we enjoy pictures of climbers conquering a summit and a marathoner crossing the finish line with her arms in the air but we don't aspire to join them. *Watching* the Olympics is one thing. *Participating* and going for gold is another matter entirely. Angela Duckworth cites the example of an Olympic Gold Medalist:

> We want to believe that Mark Spitz was born to swim in a way that none of us were and that none of us could. We don't want to sit on the pool deck and watch him progress from amateur to expert. We prefer our excellence fully formed. We prefer mystery to mundanity.[2]

Unless one is born into the rare privilege of wealth and influence, greatness *is* the fruit of something very mundane: hard work. Researchers have learned that success is far more about blood, sweat, and tears invested in patient, laborious practice over weeks, months, and years than it is about innate talent given as a birthright to an elite few. Malcolm Gladwell asserts that "10,000 hours is the magic number of greatness," an observation that contradicts the popular assumption that some people were born with natural talent and had an easy trip to the top of their field.[3] "Achievement is talent plus preparation," Gladwell says. "The problem . . . is, the closer psychologists look at the careers of the gifted, the smaller the role innate talent seems to play and the bigger the role preparation seems to play."[4]

In the early 1990s, psychologist K. Anders Ericsson and two colleagues at Berlin's Academy of Music conducted a study and

> couldn't find any "naturals," musicians who floated effortlessly to the top while practicing a fraction of the time their peers did. Nor could they find any "grinds," people who worked harder than everyone else, yet just didn't have what it takes to break the top ranks. Their research suggests . . . *the thing that distinguishes one performer from another is how hard he or she works. That's it.* And what's more, the people at the very top don't work harder or even much harder than everyone else. *They work much,* **much** *harder.*[5]

Christians agree that talent must be developed with hard work. We simply honor God as the originator of talents and gifts. The development of skills is a part of our faithfulness. God appoints His people to do certain things and endows us with gifts and talents for the job. Yet God also expects us to invest our lives, develop our skills, and produce increase as a way of honoring and obeying Him. Jesus told a parable about a master who went on a long journey and entrusted his servants with his wealth, some receiving more, some less, each according to his ability. When he returned, he asked them to give an account of themselves. The ones who multiplied the trusted investment were praised and rewarded. One squandered his opportunity by burying the investment in the ground. He was severely chastised and punished (Matt. 25:14–30).

MOTIVATIONS FOR SUCCESS

As human aspirations go, from a secular perspective, getting wealthy and becoming famous or powerful makes sense. For-profit corporations exist to make money, so accumulating wealth and influence is appropriate, even necessary. It seems inherent to the human psyche to better ourselves, to use our skills and talents to meet needs, to become financially stable, and through these efforts, to gain notoriety and earn the respect of our peers.

Aspiring to wealth, fame, or power can be a two-edged sword, however, depending on one's motivations. Angela Duckworth surveyed sixteen thousand people who completed her "Grit Scale" and an additional questionnaire.[6] She referenced two motivational terms, coined by the Greek philosopher Aristotle: *eudaimonic* ("in harmony with one's good . . . inner spirit") and *hedonic* ("positive, in-the-moment, inherently self-centered"). To her surprise, Duckworth discovered that many gritty people are eudaimonic. She calls this motivation "purpose—the intention to contribute to the well-being of others."[7]

> Grittier people are *dramatically* more motivated than others to seek a meaningful, other-centered life. . . . This is not to say that all grit paragons are saints, but rather, that most gritty people see their ultimate aims as deeply connected to the world beyond themselves.[8]

Duckworth conceded that she did not know the people who took part in her survey, and somewhat facetiously conceded she couldn't be sure if any terrorists participated. Her point, of course, was that not all gritty people are philanthropic. Some, like perhaps Joseph Stalin and Adolf Hitler during their lifetimes, were total hedonists and tyrants. She was just surprised to learn that many gritty people actually wanted to contribute to the well-being of others.

I had to wonder about those sixteen thousand people. Who are they? What are their underlying beliefs? What worldviews drive them? Are some of them Christians? From my observations, secular research focuses more on outward behavior and success—making money, building a company, and gaining notoriety—and less on worldviews, beliefs, and values. The focus is usually on what people do, not on their moral or existential motivations.

The "Nature-Nurture" Criteria of Success

Malcolm Gladwell adds that success is also influenced by *outside* factors such as the time, the place, and the people around a successful person. Bill Gates and Steve Jobs, for example, were both smart, young men, but neither became giants in the computer industry simply because they liked computers and were intelligent and creative. They lived in strategic places that offered access to our nation's fledgling computer industry at an important time. The fact that these men worked long hours for months and years and invested their latent interest and intelligence in the field of computer science does not detract from the fact that Seattle and Silicon Valley gave them strategic opportunities. If these men had grown up in the rural Midwest, their experiences and impact would have likely been very different.

According to Duckworth, research also shows that nature-determined and nurture-influenced realities are not static. For example, people in the United States are on average five inches taller than they were 150 years ago. This is attributed to improved living conditions and nourishment. Innate intelligence, especially the ability to do abstract reasoning, seems to be changing as well. Duckworth references "The Flynn Effect":

> Named after Jim Flynn, the New Zealand social scientist who discovered it, the Flynn Effect refers to startling gains in IQ scores over the past century. How big are the gains? On the most widely used IQ tests today . . . gains have averaged more than fifteen points in the last fifty years in the more than thirty countries that have been studied.[9]

Clinical psychologist Dr. Henry Cloud also echoes this nurture connection, saying, for good or for bad, people have extraordinary power over us. People can improve our lives and inspire us to do greater things than we would ever do on our own. They can also diminish our potential and move us toward ruin. "The undeniable reality is that how well you do in life . . . depends not only on . . . your skills and competencies, but also on who is doing it *with* you or *to* you. . . . These people are literally making you who you are."[10]

Cloud cites an example of a Navy Seal candidate—he calls

him Bryce—who must swim in open water to the shoreline to pass a final test, the culmination of "Hell Week," where aspiring SEALs are pressed to their limits and beyond.

Some of Bryce's candidate buddies had already completed the test and were standing on the beach watching their comrades in the water. That's when Bryce "hit a wall" from the debilitating effects of cold, fatigue, and stress. No matter how much he willed himself to keep going, his body would not obey. He began to sink in the water, overcome by fatigue. At this moment, his eyes fell on the beach where his candidate friend Mark was watching him struggle.

> Mark gave him a huge fist pump and a yell, signaling to Bryce that "he could do it." Their eyes locked for a few seconds, and as Bryce described it, *something* happened. *Something beyond him.* His body jumped into another gear, into another dimension of performance that he had not had access to before; he was able to get back on top of the cold water again and swim toward the finish line. He made it. He finished. He would be a SEAL. That is the "power of the other."[11]

Human aspirations for greatness have resulted in profound achievements for both individuals and society. Advances in technology, medicine, and the sciences are the product of our latent desire to accomplish, build, and learn. From the Golden Gate Bridge to the discovery of penicillin, humans have taken their curiosity and frustrations with the status quo and transformed the world. We have put men on the moon and uncovered the mysteries of DNA. Yet, with all our learning and advancement, we still struggle in our relationships. We fight each other and go to war. People kill each other over issues of greed and jealousy. Great human achievement has not awarded us everything to which we aspire. Inner peace and peace on earth continually elude us. Accomplishment still leaves us cold and unfulfilled. What is missing in the human aspiration for greatness?

In the next chapter, we will look at this important question and explore what the Bible says and what people have discovered about greatness from God's perspective.

Discussion Questions

1. On the "nature-nurture" subject, how much can you really change about yourself?
2. Have you identified your latent skills and talents? If not, how do you plan to discover them? If you have, what are you doing to develop them further?
3. Who in your life can help you develop your aspirations?
4. What might be holding you back from pursuing your aspirations and how will you address the challenge?

5

GREATNESS FROM GOD'S PERSPECTIVE

We must repudiate this great, modern wave of seeking God
for His benefits. The sovereign God wants to be loved for
Himself and honored for Himself, but that is only part of what
He wants. The other part is that He wants us to know that
when we have Him, we have everything—we have all the rest.

—A. W. TOZER [1]

Joey Buran was introduced to surfing when he was twelve years
old. A short time later, he saw the Billabong Pipeline Masters
on television. He told his parents, "I'm going to win the Pipeline Masters." That dream became a driving force in Joey's life
and he was soon dominating the Southern California surf
scene. When he was seventeen, Joey competed in the Billabong
Pipeline Masters on the North Shore of Oahu, Hawaii, and
took fifth place in the finals. The achievement made him the
youngest competitor in history to be a Pipe Masters finalist.

Newly dubbed "The California Kid," Joey Buran spent

the next four years on the ASP World Tour. In 1984, Joey returned to the Pipeline Masters tournament. In the final heat, he caught a set wave and clinched the win. Standing on the podium in front of thousands of adoring fans, waving the Pipe Masters Trophy above his head, Joey shouted, "Dreams come true, man! All I got to say, dreams come true!" With the declaration echoing in the air, and Joey still waving the trophy above his head, a huge torrent of wind and rain blew in, pummeling the crowd, the stage, and the entire beach. Everybody ran for cover. An official came up and took the treasured trophy from Joey's hands; it is a perpetual trophy so he was not allowed to take it home. The trophy, the officials, and the entire crowd disappeared into a haze of rain, wind, and sand.

"I was standing all alone on the beach at Pipeline," Joey later remembered. "It was the most empty moment of my life. And I thought, 'This is it?'"[2] After an incredible win, a dream that had driven his life for a decade, Joey was left standing alone on a drenched stage forced to confront the fickle nature of human glory. In the months that followed, he fell into depression. He began doing drugs and drinking heavily. After a drug overdose and suicide attempt, Joey sought help. His journey led him to a transforming encounter with Jesus Christ. Today, Joey serves as a pastor in Southern California.

The first question that comes to mind in Joey's story is, "Why did this incredible win, a decade-long dream now fulfilled, end so poorly?" The answer lies in what drives everyone who aspires for greatness: our motivations. Externally, Joey Buran reached for a dream and made it come true. Internally, the achievement did not deliver what he expected. What then was Joey Buran's greatest achievement? Some might say winning the Pipeline Masters was Joey Buran's apex accomplishment. Others might point to the moment when he confronted depression and addiction and pursued a path to overcome them. Each of these certainly were notable achievements. But Joey would undoubtedly say his life's greatest accomplishment had nothing to do with what he did. It was what Jesus Christ did for him. His greatest moment in life was meeting Jesus Christ and committing his life to following Him.

WHAT IS TRUE GREATNESS?

Christians are appropriately cautious about wealth, fame, and power as ends in themselves. We strive for something of higher importance and value, for God's glory and the advancement of the gospel. Wealth, fame, and power can serve this purpose, but are not essential. A pastor friend recently remarked, "In the end, the only recognition that matters is Jesus."[3]

What then is greatness in God's eyes? Greatness begins with humility and a commitment to Jesus Christ, to become the person He calls us to be, and to be on His mission. Our best work is to seek the glory and centrality of God and to be faithful to His assignment. A Christ-centered person is committed to put God first and to seek His greatness, for God's glory to be known, and His purposes to be advanced. If we become great by human standards, it is only for His glory and His mission. If we accomplish great things, we did it because God empowered us to advance His purposes on the earth. At the core, we don't care about public acknowledgment or reward. We accept it graciously when it comes to us, but we are not seeking it, and don't need it to define ourselves. We are in the service of Jesus Christ, and are therein content. God gets the glory, and that is enough for us. About Christian service expectations, Count Zinzendorf once stated, "You must be content to suffer, to die, and to be forgotten."[4]

The Bible and Aspirations for Greatness

When Jesus is at the center of our lives, we are positioned for God's greatness. Why? *Because God can trust us* with His investment. We will be tested, but as we walk in faithfulness, God will fulfill His purposes in our lives! A person who is satisfied wholly with God's glory will happily redirect acclaim back to Him. It would be unnatural to squander glory on ourselves. A trustworthy Christian never forgets God's gracious salvation, how He delivered us from sin. We are grateful for God's abiding grace in our lives. The apostle Paul lived continually with a deep sense of indebtedness:

> For I am the least of the apostles, unworthy to be called an apostle, because I persecuted the church of God. But by the grace of God I am what I am, and his grace toward me was not in vain. On the contrary, I worked harder than any of them, though it was not I, but the grace of God that is with me. (1 Cor. 15:9–10)

God seeks trustworthy people who will think big, pray big, and work for big goals for His glory, knowing that it is

God at work in and through them, and that only through Him will things of enduring value ever happen.

As a young adult, missionary pioneer William Carey was a poor shoemaker in England. God gave him a vision for the unreached nations of the world, and by faithful, patient service over a lifetime, he became a catalyst for a Christian movement in India. He completed Bible translations in six Indian languages, he made disciples and planted churches, he built Christian education institutions, and he advocated for the abolition of the practice of "suttee" (wife burning). Today Carey is remembered as the father of modern missions.

If the biblical narrative tells us anything, if we learn anything from Christian history, we learn that God uses common people to do His work. They are not wise or powerful or of noble birth by the world's standards, but they believe God's Word is true and the Great Commission is serious business. They get stuff done because they lean on God and expect Him to do great things. God responds to their daring faith and glorifies Himself through their humble obedience. A. W. Tozer said,

> We must repudiate this great, modern wave of seeking
> God for His benefits. The sovereign God wants to be
> loved for Himself and honored for Himself, but that
> is only part of what He wants. The other part is that
> He wants us to know that when we have Him, *we have
> everything—we have all the rest.*[5]

Jesus essentially said the same thing. "But seek ye first the kingdom of God, and his righteousness; *and all these things shall be added unto you*" (Matt. 6:33 KJV). There is a sad futility in aspiring to greatness without reference to God's purposes. The human yearning for achievement, money, position, and influence is ultimately unfulfilling and has no enduring value when God is disregarded. While external success might be achieved, the thrill of the conquest, the adoration of the crowds, and the feeling of satisfaction slips away. The elation of success wanes. The crowds move on.

For a Christian, aspirations for greatness have important implications. While aspirations are common to every person—they drive our choices, activities, education, friendships, and where we live and work—a Christian wants to know what God has to say about these things and how our aspirations advance God's purposes and the Great Commission of Jesus Christ. We ask God to guide us both in the big-picture questions about the future, and in the small details we face right now. God calls us to do great things for Him, but that call begins with an aspiration to be a godly person, to become like Jesus in faith, in humility, and in character. This is the fountainhead of all outward forms of Christian achievement and greatness.

NATURE–NURTURE AND THE BIBLE

Angela Duckworth identified both the "nature" (genetic) and "nurture" (external) influences attributable to human achievement.[6] As Christians we agree in part with Duckworth's assessment. But we go back one step further: God designed our genetic makeup and He guides us in our external influences.

For you formed my inward parts;
  you knitted me together in my mother's womb.
I praise you, for *I am fearfully and wonderfully made.*
Wonderful are your works;
  my soul knows it very well.
My frame was not hidden from you,
when I was being made in secret,
  intricately woven in the depths of the earth.
Your eyes saw my unformed substance;
in your book were written, every one of them,
    the days that were formed for me,
    when as yet there was none of them. (Ps. 139:13–16)

God designs our entire being—our physical, emotional, mental, and spiritual makeup. He alone gives us gifts. He instills within each person certain interests, inclinations, and latent skills. The fact that we must identify and nurture these gifts and develop our skills, and that we have responsibility in the process, is also a miracle of His grace at work within us. We cultivate our gifts as an expression of faith, obedience, and gratitude.

The journey begins with a hunger for spiritual maturity: to know God and be grounded in Him, to be set apart for His purposes, and from that foundation, to discover our spiritual gifts. One of life's most exciting experiences is the discovery of how God has graciously gifted us. To know you love music, or science, or art, or languages. To discover you love to teach and nurture young hearts and minds. To become aware that God uniquely formed you to work with information (as a historian, researcher, mathematician, teacher, or attorney), or with people (as a family doctor or counselor or pastor), or with your hands (as a builder or craftsman or artist). To discover a love for cross-cultural ministry, or to teach or preach the Bible. To be an evangelist. To work with the poor. To serve the victims of injustice and offer God's gracious healing and salvation. Whether our spiritual gifts find expression in the workplace, the church, or the mission field, whether in school, on a farm, or in public service, God has an assignment for each of us.

Discovering God's gifts is the first step. Patient practice in developing those gifts and skills so that we can honorably serve Him is the longer journey. That requires perseverance. On that longer road, we discover the joy of the patient, cooperative pull where God guides our internal growth and our outward development. In the little forward steps we take through storms, disappointments, mistakes, and roadblocks, God shapes us into Christlikeness. All the while He wonderfully includes us in His work, working through imperfect beings on an imperfect journey! Paul said it this way:

> For God, who said, "Let light shine out of darkness," has shone in our hearts to give the light of the knowledge of the glory of God in the face of Jesus Christ. But we have this treasure in jars of clay, to show that the surpassing power belongs to God and not to us. (2 Cor. 4:6–7)

God is with us on our journey of spiritual formation and lifelong growth. The apostle Paul writes to the Christians in

Philippi about God's commitment to us: "And I am sure of this, that he who began a good work in you will bring it to completion at the day of Jesus Christ" (Phil. 1:6). We therefore take great hope in both our mistakes *and* our successes, knowing God is working in us and through us. Difficulties build character, prove passion, and shape our lives, forming Christ in us. In the end, the mature servant, who faithfully walked with God, has a compelling testimony that inspires others, whose gifts, applied in humble service, have affected the world.

TOWARD POWERFUL CHRISTIAN SERVICE

In the introduction, I told a story about WC. WC's mentor was an evangelist named Ray Jennings. In the late 1960s, Ray Jennings took his family to India to preach the gospel. Within a decade, he had preached to millions of people. In the early 1980s, India's prime minister, Indira Gandhi, invited Ray Jennings and his team to conduct an open-air event in the heart of New Delhi. A friend of mine, who was on the Jennings team, has a picture of Ray standing beside India's prime minister—one of the most powerful women in the world—flanked by team members in the backyard of her home. It was a high honor, and Ray Jennings graciously accepted it. But he probably did not consider the experience a defining moment in his life. Why? Because Ray Jennings wanted something else.

Ray Jennings wanted to bring the gospel to millions of people. It did not matter to him whether his success in that quest included personal fame or recognition. In fact, he resisted such distinctions. His journey in India started simply and quietly. In the beginning, Ray preached in Indian churches, knowing no other way to build a ministry. In time, however, he became frustrated. "I don't want to preach only inside of church buildings," Ray complained in prayer. "Millions do not know about Jesus! I want to be outside with the lost, preaching to them!" He sought God fervently. Finally, God spoke to him in a whisper, with eight simple words: "Go to the open fields like I did." That simple guidance changed everything. Ray and his oldest son, Phillip, began going to remote villages where they could preach the good news about Jesus Christ in the open air. They invited people to receive Jesus as Savior and Lord. They prayed for the people, including the sick and oppressed. And, within a short time, they were preaching to multitudes.

The Jennings family knew extreme heartbreak too. When he was in his late teens, Phillip began traveling regularly with his father, helping in the work. A few years later, Phillip tragically died in an accident. The excruciating grief that followed Phillip's death pressed heavily on the Jennings family. At one point, Ray felt as though Satan would crush the ministry. But the family endured through their sorrow and found God's grace. They stayed in Asia and continued preaching. The work did not die. In fact, it grew.

In 1982, after our internship with WC, our family joined the Jennings team in India for a year. I observed with my own eyes Christ's compassion for the multitudes, and how the Holy Spirit would do miraculous things to reveal Jesus to people. It's hard to put into words, but somehow, it seemed that Ray's simple carefulness to give God all the glory, and his simple boldness to proclaim the gospel, was pleasing to God, and He just showed up. There were two other keys to Ray's success: his deep love for the poor in the villages of India, and his refusal to quit doing difficult work in a very remote part of the world. Ray called this quality "stick-to-itiveness." His love for India drove him to prayer. Our team prayed for two hours every day. At other times, we could hear Ray, behind closed doors, quietly weeping in prayer. I learned how to weep for the lost by spending a year with this man. God did something big in my heart just by being around him.

Ray Jennings never sought the world's greatness. His goal was the greatness of God and the love of Jesus Christ in the hearts of people. His method was the preaching of the gospel. In part, Ray Jennings sought the glory of God through anonymity. He never published his name on ministry advertising. He never allowed pictures to be taken in his meetings. He never published a book or magazine. He was not wealthy, and, compared to earthly fame, he was loved and honored by only a few. But today, perhaps millions of people will be in heaven because of his faithful, persevering service for the cause of Christ and the glory of God.

In our journey of faith, to overcome the things that drag us down, to become mature in Christ, and to accomplish what He has called us to do, we lean into God, we trust His Word, and we get help and encouragement from God's people. Through His unlimited power and presence in our lives, and through the wisdom of His people, God provides what we need to be and do what He has planned for us. The apostle Paul emphasizes this principle to the Philippian church.

Not that I have already obtained this or am already perfect, *but I press on to make it my own*, because Christ Jesus has made me his own. Brothers, I do not consider that I have made it my own. But one thing I do: forgetting what lies behind and *straining forward to what lies ahead, I press on toward the goal* for the prize of the upward call of God in Christ Jesus. (Phil. 3:12–14)

God asks His people to turn our backs on temporal quests and earthly acclaim and turn to pursuing the glory of God. When we aspire to the higher purposes of our living Savior, we will discover true greatness. God will meet our needs and God will make us great in His sight. Whether through abundant success or in loneliness and tragedy, God will bring us to the completion of His purposes.

No, in all these things we are more than conquerors through him who loved us. For I am sure that neither death nor life, nor angels nor rulers, nor things present nor things to come, nor powers, nor height nor depth, nor anything else in all creation, will be able to separate us from the love of God in Christ Jesus our Lord. (Rom. 8:37–39)

There is an important lesson for us in the Ray Jennings story. When we expect God to do great things through our lives, and allow Him to work in us even in times of loss and difficult experiences that seem like setbacks, when we lean into His grace and trust Him, our grief does not harden us. Rather,

God builds something profound within us. He exponentially increases our love for people by giving us His compassion for those who suffer. Because we ourselves have suffered, because we have faced difficulty and learned to lean into Jesus Christ in our pain, we understand what others go through. We gain Christ's gentle empathy for them. The reason Ray Jennings could weep with compassion for the people of India is in part the result of his own losses, and his experience with the comforting work of the Holy Spirit. God gave Ray Jennings a great love for India, a love that grew through his own sufferings and losses and the comfort he had received from Jesus Christ.

These things are the foundations of God's greatness! They are also the essence of what we will consider next: Moral Courage—where God sometimes allows us to experience great difficulty on our journey of obedience, and through suffering He leads us into the fulfillment of His higher purposes.

Discussion Questions

1. How do you balance a desire for approval from others with being content with approval from God alone?
2. What "great aspiration" might God be envisioning for your life and what should you do to prepare for it?
3. What is your biggest fear in being obedient to God's calling?

6

MORAL COURAGE

By faith Noah, being warned by God concerning
events as yet unseen, in reverent fear constructed
an ark for the saving of his household.

HEBREWS 11:7

The Noah's ark narrative is the first story in the Bible that records great moral courage. God commanded Noah to steward
the future of the human race by building a ship the likes of
which had never been seen before. He was expected to *believe*
an impossible story about coming global destruction-by-flood
and then *act* by constructing an intricately designed seago-
ing craft that would save eight human beings . . . and a lot of
animals. Here are the opening instructions from God to Noah,
and Noah's response:

> "I have determined to make an end of all flesh, for the
> earth is filled with violence through them. Behold, I will
> destroy them with the earth. Make yourself an ark of
> gopher wood. Make rooms in the ark, and cover it inside

and out with pitch. . . ." Noah did this; he did all that God
commanded him. (Gen. 6:13–14, 22)

Not only was the prediction given to Noah unbelievable
to most and the task next to impossible, God expected Noah
to build a ridiculous monstrosity for no imminent reason.
The Bible is silent about whether or not Noah was mocked
by the wider community as he worked. It does say he was a
"preacher of righteousness" (2 Peter 2:5 NIV). How and what
he preached is unknown, but one doesn't need an imagination
to assume that the neighbors asked questions and expressed
opinions. The Genesis account is pointed in its contrasts:
Noah was righteous, he was blameless, and he walked with
God; the earth was corrupt and violent (Gen. 1:11–12).

Noah's mandate was no Everyday Endurance challenge.
This was no Aspiration for Greatness that would be rewarded
with promotions and prominence, not from Noah's point of
view at the time. The defining characteristic of the task was
saving his family, and by extension the world, from destruction
by an unprecedented global event. In human terms, Noah's
ark was an enterprise of folly on a monumental scale. Even
measured by today's standards, the ark is a marvel of technology. According to author John D. Morris, modern naval archi-
tecture confirms that the ark's design was perfect for seafaring
stability, almost impossible to capsize.

Note the ratio of length to width of the Ark's design:
300 cubits to 50 cubits, or approximately 450 feet long
to 75 feet wide. This ratio of six-to-one is well known in

naval design for optimum stability. Many modern naval engineers, when designing cargo ships to battleships, utilize this same basic design ratio.[1]

Noah was 480 years old when God asked him to build the ark. One hundred and twenty years later, the ark was complete, and God's hand closed its side door. Sealed within its bowels was the consummate menagerie: every living thing that crawled, walked, and flew—perhaps as many as eight thousand different animal kinds, doubled for pairs—plus eight members of Noah's family.[2]

At the appointed time, "all the fountains of the great deep burst forth, and the windows of the heavens were opened. And rain fell upon the earth forty days and forty nights" (Gen. 7:11–12). What an ominous day! Water burst from every pore of the earth, torrents crashed from above, and floodwaters surged everywhere. Yet, thanks to Noah's obedience, the ark's human and animal cargo were safe.

It is hard to get our heads around such a monumental feat: one hundred and twenty years of preparation, and a labor of patient obedience until an unprecedented project was completed, one that preserved the future of humanity and all creation.

THE SOURCE OF MORAL COURAGE

The book of Hebrews retells the Noah story among others, commending the biblical heroes for their moral courage. Hebrews tells us that each person *saw* or was *looking for* something. Noah was warned by God "concerning events *as yet unseen*" (Heb. 11:7). Abraham went out, "not knowing where he was going," but he was "*looking forward* to a city that has foundations, whose designer and builder is God" (Heb. 11:8–10). Moses "was *looking to* the reward" (Heb. 11:26). These heroes of faith "*saw promises*" and greeted them "from afar." They "desired a better country," not one that was bound to earth and dirt, and blood and breath, but "a heavenly one" (Heb. 11:13–16).

Joseph, who is mentioned briefly in the book of Hebrews (11:21–22), had a God-given dream in which he *saw* future events. The youthful dream was severely tested. He was betrayed by his brothers, sold as a slave, and carried to Egypt. He was falsely accused; he languished in prison. But then, after many years, the dream was powerfully fulfilled.[3] Writer Mary Fairchild comments, "Joseph is one of the greatest heroes of the Old Testament and an extraordinary example of what can happen when a person surrenders his life in complete obedience to God."[4] Hebrews 11:32–38 reaches a crescendo of moral courage with words like these:

> Gideon, Barak, Samson . . . who through faith conquered kingdoms, enforced justice, obtained promises, stopped the mouths of lions, quenched the power of fire, escaped the edge of the sword. . . . Others . . . destitute, afflicted, mistreated—of whom the world was not worthy.

German philosopher and atheist Friedrich Nietzsche said, "He who has a why to live can bear almost any how."[5] There is a poignant irony here: perhaps, for just a brief moment,

Nietzsche and Jesus agreed on something! *When we have a* **why**, *we can endure almost any* **how**. Survival in suffering is rooted in our ability to find meaning in something beyond ourselves.

For the Christian, our lives are rooted in the glory of God. John Piper wrote: *"God is most glorified in us when we are most satisfied in him.* This is perhaps the most important sentence in my theology."[6] God's glory is the connecting thread of all biblical stories. Those who experienced difficulty and endured did so because they saw something of God and His plans. Vision sustained their faith. It kept hope alive, it empowered them to obey, to press forward, to survive, and to go on as long as they could. Friedrich Nietzsche called it meaning; John Piper calls it the glory of God.

Noah saw a future beyond global disaster, and built an ark to save his family. Moses saw the end of slavery in Egypt and freedom for God's people in a new land of promise. These and other heroes of the Bible—both men and women, plus a litany of heroes throughout Christian history—saw something (see Heb. 11:32–38)! Their vision of the glory and power of God so transformed their lives, and so nourished their souls, that even in the challenges they faced, they were able to survive, to endure, to overcome. Their courage began with God. It proceeded forward by obedience. It finished with glory! What they did would have never happened without God's inspired directive and their willful obedience. None were without sin. All were flawed. All certainly faced discouragement. None obeyed perfectly. But each one found sustenance in their relationship with God and His glory.

So what exactly is the glory of God? Author and missiologist Steve Hawthorne says the Hebrew word for *glory* means "weight, substance, and at the same time brilliance or radiant beauty."[7] It could be called *vision*. It certainly implies something about human experience, something we "see" in our connections with God. It relates to how we perceive Him, how we understand God's identity, and define His work in our lives. But that is only one part of the answer. The human experience with God is not the whole of God's glory. People *see* or are touched by the glory of God when we encounter Him. But the glory of God is far bigger than our subjective experience. The Bible says:

> The heavens declare the glory of God;
>> the skies proclaim the work of his hands.
> Day after day they pour forth speech;
>> night after night they reveal knowledge.
> They have no speech, they use no words;
>> no sound is heard from them.
> Yet their voice goes out into all the earth,
>> their words to the ends of the world.
> (Ps. 19:1–4 NIV)

God's glory is His entire incomprehensible identity—His sovereignty[8] and His completeness in Himself, an eternal reality that preexists the created universe. Hawthorne continues,

> The Bible is basically a story about God. When we turn to the Bible as a self-help book, we end up bored or

frustrated with what seems to be a rambling collection
of stories. What if the Bible is more about God than it is
about us? . . . How thrilling to discover that every element
of scripture . . . converge[s] in one central saga of one
worthy Person.[9]

I was recently studying to teach a class for a course called
the Perspectives on the World Christian Movement.[10] Lesson
Two centers around Steve Hawthorne's article "The Story of
His Glory." While preparing, I was reminded of my own experience with Jesus, and what inspired our young family to
leave a comfortable life in the United States and move to the
other side of the world. Why did we do such a radical thing?
It wasn't world need that inspired us to go, although that was
a part of the decision. We were aware of the challenges of
Asia. We loved the idea of serving God in the most densely
populated region of the world. But what inspired us was
something else.

I was eighteen when I surrendered my life to Jesus, an
aimless teenager who became tired of the excesses of a generation who grew up in the 1960s. The Jesus Movement started
in those days. Christian leaders began reaching out to young
people with a message of hope through Jesus Christ. Friends
and praying parents invited (almost dragged) me to a Christian rally where I was confronted with the transforming power
of the gospel. I had heard it all before, but this time, the words
of Jesus to Nicodemus grabbed ahold of my troubled heart (see
John 3:1–21). For the first time in my life, Jesus' words made
sense. "If you want to change the world, you have to start with

you! You must be born again!" the preacher said. I sat on a hill with ten thousand young people gathered on a Pennsylvania farmer's field and prayed, "That's what I want."

To this day, I can't explain what happened that night. I was lost but now I am found. I was dead but now I am alive. The metaphors of Scripture seek to explain the mystery of the new birth, but words cannot convey the meaning entirely. The glory of God is sort of like that. The way we experience Him is deeply personal and internal, yet huge and good and transformative and ultimately bigger than us. It is transcendent. The Holy Spirit comes to us, fills us with Himself, washes us clean in the cleansing blood of Jesus Christ, and then He just overflows into our lives. It's the glory of God! We instinctively know we have tapped into something big, but it really is beyond description. Words alone cannot capture the entire meaning and weight of God's glory. But one thing we know: when we encounter Him, His glory transforms our lives and inspires us to be courageous and do exploits that in themselves are beyond our abilities or inclinations.

GOING WITH JESUS ON MISSION

Adoniram Judson was touched by the glory of God.[11] As a young man, Judson first rejected the claims of Christianity, and then, when one of his friends died, he saw his own sin and arrogance. Judson surrendered to Jesus Christ and was transformed by the power of the gospel. A short time later he committed his life to take the gospel to Asia. That decision meant Judson became one of North America's first Protestant missionaries. In 1812, twenty-three-year-old Adoniram and his wife, Ann, and six colleagues left New England for India. Upon arrival many months later, what had started as an aspiration for greatness in mission became a challenge of moral courage as their colleagues and their children died one after the other from tropical diseases. The Judsons lost their first two children, then when their third, Maria, was two years old, Ann died. Little Maria followed her mother to the grave six months later.

Adoniram married again, to Sarah Boardman, the widow of another missionary. In the years following, Adoniram and Sarah had eight children. Two died in infancy. When Sarah fell ill, Adoniram boarded a boat and rushed her back to the United States for medical treatment. Sarah died on the journey. Adoniram arrived in Boston a broken, middle-aged man. Eventually Judson met a young Christian writer named Emily Chubbock who offered to help him write his memoirs. They married and the couple returned to Burma. Three years later, when Adoniram was sixty-one years old, he became seriously ill. He died on a sailing voyage seeking medical help and was buried at sea in the Indian Ocean.

Adoniram Judson had spent more than three decades in Burma. He lost two wives and five children. But he had also accomplished great things for Christ and the Burmese people. He mastered the Burmese language and translated the entire Bible from the original Hebrew and Greek into Burmese. To this day, Judson's Burmese Bible is the only translation in use in Burma. Judson courageously introduced the Burmese people to Jesus Christ. The Burmese church was born by his patient service;

it continues to grow today. In some districts of this staunchly Buddhist land, the Burmese church continues to flourish.

Against the influences of contemporary secular culture, it is difficult to understand such commitment and perseverance. Did the Judson family follow God's call or were they impetuous fools? Was their vision worth the suffering and loss they endured? Today, we are accustomed to ease and safety, even in global mission. Compared to the dangers the Judson family endured, a lot of mission work today is a walk in the park. The planet has been tamed. We expect ease and comfort. They expected hardship and danger. We expect to live a long life and come home healthy. They expected to die on the field. We assume protection is a part of biblical Christianity. They assumed danger, even death, was their lot in life. We are unfamiliar with hardship. They knew it as a constant companion.

On one hand, we are grateful for the safety and prosperity of the modern world. On the other, we would be wise to question how much we expect ease, comfort, and safety to be a part of our fulfillment of God's purposes. Could God ask us to go somewhere or do something that includes suffering? To contract disease? To lay down our lives? I admire the Judson family. In the face of incredible odds, great loss, and sometimes appalling treatment, they did not quit. I admire the women who served beside Adoniram Judson. These strong, gifted women were filled with vision of their own. Ann Judson opened doors in Burma with her amicable personality. Her Esther-like boldness in approaching and befriending Burmese royalty could have resulted in her death. Sarah Judson stayed in Burma after losing her first husband and all of her children, save one, and married Adoniram. She could have quit and gone home. But, together with her second husband, she pursued their God-given vision, even in terrible loss and grief, and stuck to the task they had received. The Judson family gave their lives for the Burmese people and walked out a bold vision to plant the gospel in a faraway land. That work is still bearing fruit today. Might God ask the same from us?

THE POWER BEHIND PERSEVERANCE

The more I have studied perseverance and have had to persevere through my own difficulties, the more I have come to believe that the most powerful force for the advancement of the gospel is God's determined people, and the most powerful force behind them is the glory of God. We cannot endure for long on our own. But we can do all things through Christ who gives us strength (Phil. 4:13)! Even with the unsupportive influences of culture, we can follow Jesus Christ in His mission! Jesus empowers us. Jesus gives us grace.

Morally courageous people perceive something that is more vivid than the rising sun, and more inspiring than a brilliant night sky. They have experienced God's glory revealed in Jesus Christ, a love and nearness that flows through their lives in witness and service. That connection with God's Son is grounded in intimacy with God's Word and His Holy Spirit. Their enduring strength is founded on God's eternal truth and His boundless love. We too, when we have experienced God's glory, can forgive, endure, and move patiently forward in faith. God's glory as revealed in Jesus Christ helps us serve even when we hurt and our work seems pointless. Paul had this to say about the glory of God:

> For our light affliction, which is but for a moment, is working for us a far more exceeding and eternal weight of glory, while we do not look at the things which are seen, but at the things which are not seen. For the things which are seen are temporary, but the things which are not seen are eternal. (2 Cor. 4:17–18 NKJV)

Jesus shared the same theme with His disciples only hours before Calvary. "Father, the hour has come; glorify your Son that the Son may glorify you. . . . I glorified you on earth, having accomplished the work that you gave me to do" (John 17:1–4). Jesus framed His brutal death on a Roman cross as God's work to glorify God. The glory was not escaping death; it was entering it. In the same way, the glory of God is the fuel for us to have moral courage in the face of every difficulty. It empowers us to face personal loss, whether that be death of a loved one, the devastation of a broken relationship, or the end of a career. It is the driving force of all Christian service and of sacrificial living. It fuels obedience and faithfulness to God like nothing else and keeps God's people moving forward in obedience even when they might face humanity's most difficult experiences. Perseverance is not just about being "in ministry" or being a "missionary." It is about being on mission with Jesus Christ, being in love with Him and committed to His purposes in school, on the job, in marriage, and in our communities. John Piper says to Christian leaders:

When the glory of God himself saturates our preaching . . . and when he predominates above our talk of methods and strategies . . . then the people might begin to feel that he is the central reality of their lives, and that the spread of his glory is more important than all their possessions and all their plans.[12]

But the fact is, all of us, not just those in ministry, are called to be morally courageous. No one—leader, pastor, entrepreneur, student, janitor, doctor, pilot, soldier—can have genuine Christ-honoring moral courage in difficulty without the overflowing grace of God at work in us. When we lean into Him, and allow Him to have His way and place in our lives, when God's glory is our first and only aspiration, then Everyday Endurance is easier, Aspirations for Greatness are attainable, and Moral Courage becomes a reasonable quest. In his first letter, Peter writes to people experiencing great difficulty, beginning his letter by saying,

Blessed be the God and Father of our Lord Jesus Christ! According to his great mercy, he has caused us to be born again to a living hope . . . to an inheritance . . . kept in heaven for you. . . . In this you rejoice, *though now for a little while . . . you have been grieved by various trials,* so that . . . your faith . . . may be found to result in praise and glory and honor at the revelation of Jesus Christ. (1 Peter 1:3–7)

We cannot be morally courageous on our own. We are too selfish and self-absorbed. But when the glory of God explodes into our lives in all its power, we can persevere in what God asks us to be and what He asks us to do until He fulfills His purposes through us. In this life, we may never fully understand human sufferings and the sovereignty of God. We may never see the complete fulfillment in this life of what God promised us. But God *is* working to redeem the world, and we are called to participate with Him in it. Our participation includes suffering, and we, like the biblical heroes of faith and Christian servants of history, can persevere through difficulty, disappointment, even death. In the end, we glorify God by our faithfulness and our steadfast belief that He will bring His purposes to completion.

In the next chapter, we will explore how God's people are motivated to persevere even in the uncertain and tumultuous times before Christ's return and in light of eternity.

Discussion Questions

1. How should seeing God's glory inspire every Christian and make them morally courageous?
2. Are difficulties that require moral courage always involuntary, or can you volunteer for a morally courageous task?
3. How can you build courage into your life in a more intentional way in order to glorify God?

7

PERSEVERANCE AND GOD'S CONSUMMATE PURPOSES

"Now when these things begin to take place, straighten up and raise your heads, because your redemption is drawing near."

—JESUS (Luke 21:28)

When we think about the return of Jesus Christ and the consummation of all things, too often perhaps we are tempted to focus on the negative events surrounding this eschatological time in world history. Scripture is explicitly predictive on the subject of final things, and there are enough disturbing details to concern everyone. But bad news is not the point of biblical eschatology. A. W. Tozer says this about the Bible's final eschatological message:

> We have sensed the importance of John's vision in the Revelation. We are assured that God is alive and well and

that He has never abdicated His throne. While others may wonder and speculate concerning God's place in the universe . . . the Christian believer, related to God by faith, is assured of final victory. Even in the midst of earthly trials, he or she is joyful.[1]

Christians appropriately take a long view of life, and in so doing, view the end times predictions of Scripture through the lens of God's eternal plans. According to Jesus, the last days are "birth pains," a kind of temporary awfulness that precedes the glorious arrival of a new life. Even now, all creation is "pregnant" with anticipation of God's fully realized redemption (Matt. 24:8; Rom. 8:22–23). And like all healthy pregnancies, the gestation period eventually comes to full term. Contractions are the final warning that the long-awaited and greatly anticipated child is about to arrive. There may be apprehension because the mother-to-be anticipates discomfort and pain, but there is rarely terror associated with this event. Why? Because joyful expectation displaces fear. The woman endures the birth process, however unpleasant it is, for the sheer delight of the anticipated child. In the same way, Christians look forward to the return of Jesus even while we know some of the events accompanying His return will be difficult.

Like every kind of perseverance, the key to endurance in labor before "birth" is a grand expectation: a vision for something we don't yet have but passionately long for and eagerly await. We view God's kingdom rule as both now *and* not yet. We see it with the eyes of faith, there is ample evidence, and we know the "birth" will come in God's time. On the end-times clock, we don't know the day or the hour (Matt. 24:36). That uncertainty does not discourage us. The Scriptures tell us that, since the time of Christ, we have been in the last days.[2] This is not for us a gloomy reality, but something that compels us to live for Jesus and witness to a lost world. We live with the anticipation; we do not speculate about its specificity. We take hope in God's kingdom rule and hold to the promises of Scripture, knowing He is in control. Jesus rules now, He is here by the Holy Spirit, but His rule is not yet fully realized. So we patiently and actively wait.

During the final months of the Second World War, the United States—with support from Allied Forces—invaded the beaches of Normandy, France. June 6, 1944, is now remembered as D-Day. The D-Day invasion settled the outcome of the war in Europe. After D-Day, there was never any question about who won the war. But there were still many battles to be fought with many casualties until Germany formally surrendered a year later on May 7, 1945.

Calvary was the Christian D-Day. The cross of Jesus Christ and His resurrection changed everything in history. To this day, not everything has been made subject to Him, but that day is coming (1 Cor. 15:24–25; Heb. 2:8). The birth pains predicted by Jesus will be the last struggle before the consummation of God's kingdom rule. Perseverance is the key to victory in the waiting period. The church and the followers of Jesus who are alive at that time will be called upon to endure the final birth pains. Those who do will see, with their own eyes, the glorious arrival of the Son of God (1 Thess. 4:17; 1 John 3:2).

Like all difficult times, our faith and hope sustains us during the waiting period. Compared to the inheritance that will follow, the final contractions of the end times will be a temporary difficulty. This is why Jesus said, "Now when these things begin to take place, straighten up and raise your heads, because your redemption is drawing near" (Luke 21:28).

The predictions of Scripture remind us, not only of suffering, but of the glory to come. The difficulties will shake what can be shaken, and give the unbelieving world a final opportunity to turn to Him. God expects these difficult times to elicit our compassion for a lost world that pathetically clutches to a fading existence. The godless have nothing on which to cling but the fleeting stability and prosperity of the world around them. When the things they value begin to disappear, when everything they have depended upon for their identity, security, and happiness is falling apart, then the claims of Christ will be unveiled for their real power and significance. For Christians who are awake and prepared, the end of the age will be one of the most powerful evangelism opportunities of history.

This eschatological principle is true of all times and seasons in the human experience. Eugene Peterson says the uncertainty of life should be our highest motivation to live a Christ-honoring life—which is doubly true in the difficult times.

I don't know one thing about the future. I don't know what the next hour will hold. There may be sickness, accident . . . or world catastrophe. Before this day is over

I may have to deal with death, pain, loss, rejection. . . .
Still, despite my ignorance . . . I cheerfully persist in
living in the hope that nothing will separate me from
Christ's love.[3]

OUR MOTIVATIONS IN
LIGHT OF BIBLE PROPHECY

Bible prophecy should motivate every Christian to live every
season of life with eternity in mind and to compel our friends
and neighbors to awaken to life's temporal reality. All creation
testifies to this, groaning in labor over God's promised and
coming redemption (Rom. 8:22–23). Whether Christ's return
will happen in our lifetime or far in the future, we are commanded by Scripture to live expectantly, waiting and prepared
for His arrival. We are compelled to urge others to do the same.
This was Jesus' essential message about the end of the age:
"This gospel of the kingdom will be proclaimed throughout
the whole world as a testimony to all nations, and then the end
will come" (Matt. 24:14).

Jesus said in the last days, in the midst of global uncertainty,
the gospel will make an unprecedented advance around the
world. False prophets and deception, pervasive wars and global
conflicts, and famines and earthquakes in various places will
be the ominous distinctives of this time. Lawlessness will be
so widespread that the hearts of many will grow cold and fail
them for fear (see Matt. 24:12; Luke 21:25–26). Yet, according
to Jesus, God's people will not be discouraged by the trouble.
Rather, they will be empowered by it! In the middle of global

upheaval, they will go around the world, taking the gospel to every tribe and nation on earth. While the world collapses into chaos, God's people will serve and proclaim the good news! Jesus doubles down on this point, saying the gospel will be proclaimed "throughout the whole world" as a testimony "to all nations" (Matt. 24:14). After God's people have completed this profound and courageous work, then the end will come.

Christian work isn't easy even in the best of times. The reality of pervasive global sin makes our commitment to Jesus an uphill climb. God's grace is our only refuge. And a powerful one it is. But even in good times, human life is short. Eternity awaits us all, just beyond our seven or eight decades. This compels followers of Jesus to share Christ with people. During the end times, Christian work will be even more difficult. Yet, ironically, it will exponentially increase. Christians will boldly confront sin and societal decay on a grand scale and at great personal risk!

It is disingenuous for us to think our struggles are unique. This is especially true for Western Christians who, in the aggregate, enjoy the most wealth, stability, safety, health, and ease on the planet. The Western world has enjoyed over seventy years of relative peace. While we are grateful for the stability, we must be careful not to think good times will go on forever, or that when times get tough for us, the end is near. There are people in the world right now who are experiencing excruciating difficulty—war, famine, disease, poverty, starvation. All human history has reflected the Bible's eschatological message: the world is broken, but God has never abandoned us. His plans for redemption and justice are in place and moving forward. Eric Metaxas writes about what Dietrich Bonhoeffer and the German nation experienced during Hitler's reign of terror:

> Then came June 6, 1941, and the notorious Commissar Order . . . instructed the army to shoot and kill all captured Soviet military leaders. Hitler had allowed the army to avoid the most gruesome horrors in Poland. . . . But now he ordered the army itself to carry out the butchery and sadism in contravention of all military codes. . . .
>
> . . . "In the East," he said, "harshness is kindness toward the future." The leaders of the German military "must demand of themselves the sacrifice of overcoming their scruples."[4]

Hitler's sadism lies in stark contrast to what Dietrich Bonhoeffer and his colleagues were attempting to do for the German nation and church in the same period:

> In August [1941] [Bonhoeffer] wrote another circular letter to the hundred or so former [candidates for ordination]. . . . "Today I must inform you that [four of] our brothers [. . .] have been killed on the eastern front. . . . They have gone before us on the path that we shall all have to take at some point. [. . .]
>
> [. . .] Does not the early death of young Christians always appear to us as if God were plundering his own best instruments in a time in which they are most needed? Yet the Lord makes no mistakes. [. . .] Whomever God calls home is someone God has loved."[5]

Bonhoeffer later suffered greatly in prison for his resistance to the Nazi machine and was ultimately executed for alleged involvement in a plot against the regime. His final recorded words, said to a friend, were, "This is the end. For me the beginning of life."[6]

We must not kid ourselves about sin and human suffering. Those who "endure to the end" will not survive because they fled to safety or stockpiled food in their basements (Matt. 24:13).[7] We today, like those who will one day endure the earth's end time contractions, are commanded to proclaim Jesus Christ to the ends of the earth, beginning with our own neighbors. The overcoming faith and survival of God's people in every age is their connection to an almighty God who shelters us in the "shadow of [His] wings" (Ps. 17:8–9). Ultimate safety is found in only one place: a wholehearted abandonment to the purposes of God.

THE REALITY OF ETERNITY

The subject of eternity, especially the subject of hell, is a conundrum. On one hand, Christians look forward to heaven. On the other, we are reticent about the finality of hell for nonbelievers. The Bible is clear about both realities. Beginning in Genesis, the Bible records how God's creation of humanity was an eternal extension of Himself. God created us "in his own image" (Gen. 1:27). He breathed into Adam's nostrils, filling the first man's lungs with "the breath of life" (Gen. 2:7). The Genesis narrative is profound in its specificity. No other life form is called a "living being." No other part of creation was "made in God's image" and "likeness." These characteristics point to the unique *eternal* nature of human beings. This eternal feature of the human soul is our definitive "like God" attribute. Simply put, human beings cannot die.

The doctrines of an eternal heaven and hell logically follow. For Christians, heaven and hell are fundamental motivations that grow from our understanding about two things: the eternal nature of the human soul, and the reality of God's judgment on sin. I therefore care about the state of my soul; I also care about the same in others. David Platt comments,

> True belief in both heaven and hell radically changes the way we live on earth. We are encouraged by the hope of heaven, and we are compelled by the horror of hell. We know that this world is not all that exists. We know that every person on the planet is only here for a brief moment, and an eternity lies ahead of us all—an eternity that is either filled with ever-increasing delight or never-ending damnation.[8]

Heaven is God's realm. It is filled with Him in every corner. For Christians, heaven is a place of overwhelming adoration of the One who is at the center of all things and who gives meaning to everything. This is why Christians look forward to heaven. We love God, and He is there. On the flip side, it is disingenuous to claim hell cannot exist because we are uncomfortable with the idea of eternal suffering. Hell is the logical consequence of a person's refusal of God. Hell is simply God's reasonable response to someone who rejects

God and says to Him, "I love something else or someone else more than You."

The question always arises, "But what about those who have never heard the gospel? Is it just for God to allow them to suffer an eternal hell when they had no chance to hear about salvation in Jesus?" This is a difficult question, because for every plausible explanation there may always be an equally plausible exception. Yet we cannot forget God's common grace! He has clearly revealed to everyone "his invisible attributes, namely, his eternal power and divine nature . . . since the creation of the world, in the things that have been made" (Rom. 1:20). Paul precedes this declaration by saying, "For what can be known about God is plain to them, because God has shown it to them" (Rom. 1:19). The Psalms originate this idea in a profound way:

> The heavens proclaim the glory of God.
> > The skies display his craftsmanship.
> Day after day they continue to speak;
> > night after night they make him known.
> They speak without a sound or word;
> > their voice is never heard.
> Yet their message has gone throughout the earth,
> > and their words to all the world.
> (Ps. 19:1–4 NLT)

C. S. Lewis remarked, "I am not going to try to prove the doctrine [of hell] tolerable. Let us make no mistake, it is not tolerable. But I think the doctrine can be shown to be moral."[9]

We are wise to trust God and lean on Him with these questions. God is consummately fair and just. He has absolute objectivity and is not whimsical or arbitrary. We must be careful, lest we are guilty of the very indictment—of indifference and injustice—that we might lay at God's feet. In other words, do we care enough about people to share the gospel with them and get involved in their lives? God's judgments were never made from a comfortable, inactive distance. God got involved with humanity. Will we do the same? The essence of God's gritty involvement is woven into the very fabric of creation and is the story of the entire narrative of Scripture.

The cosmos is integrated. Healthy communities are integrated. A healthy body is integrated. When our physical integration breaks down, we get sick. Because a community is integrated, it is impossible to talk about justice without talking about the integrated fabric of society. Murderers kill. Robbers steal. Liars lie and slander. People's actions have consequences; they break the fabric of society. This is what we call injustice. It is not unjust, nor is it unkind, to call evil by its name. We rightly demand punishment for perpetrators. We intuitively understand that justice is necessary to restore balance to the fabric of society.

In the same way, God has set a standard—perfection and holiness—and that standard demands justice. God's justice, including His offers of mercy and redemption to the repentant heart, does not happen in idleness or detachment. God got involved in the fabric of human experience! This is the essence of His actions at the end of the age, but in fact, God's redemptive involvement started at the beginning of creation and has continued ever since. Missiologists call this a theology of mission. *God is on a mission* to bring justice to humanity, including forgiveness and redemption to all who turn to Him. It started with God walking in the garden of Eden in search of Adam and Eve, and followed with promises He made to them after the fall. It was repeated to Noah, then to Abraham when God declared that "in you all nations of the earth will be blessed" (Gen. 12:1–3). This "on mission" theme continues through the Old Testament narrative and finally reaches its culmination in Jesus Christ.

Jesus Christ identified intimately with the torn fabric of society: born in utter poverty, raised in controversy and obscurity, the presumed illegitimate son of adulterous parents who lived in a landlocked nothing town called Nazareth. When He started his ministry, Jesus lived among commoners, mostly as a drifter. He cared about sinners, the poor, and the marginalized. He defended them against the ruling class and called them His friends. All of this was God's justice and redemption at work: the incarnational reality of Immanuel, God with us.

In the end, Jesus surrendered to His enemies and suffered consummate injustice. He was arrested under false pretenses, accused by liars, beaten illegally, humiliated in a mock trial, lynched by a raging mob, counted among criminals, and hung naked on a cross built for convicts. After He died, He was taken down and buried in someone else's tomb. Yet, in all this unjust treatment, God's plan of redemption was not thwarted but in fact was fulfilled!

Here's the pressing question: In our musings about God's

justice, mercy, and involvement with people, have we done anything that remotely resembles what Jesus did? The very essence of our call to persevere is a call to serve others in Jesus' name, to be like Him, to lay our lives down for other people as He did, and to make Him known no matter what the cost might be to us personally. When the gospel is seen for what it really is—the unreserved sacrifice of Jesus Christ—it becomes impossible to believe God has not treated humankind fairly or that He is indifferent to the human dilemma. He has commissioned His entire family of followers to disseminate the message! In word and deed, we are His ambassadors!

At the end of the age, there will be a sorting of people who stand on both sides of the gospel question. In short, when we see the love of God for what it really is, our existential and theological questions are answered, if not by complete explanation, by assurance that God is just and fair. Jesus' Great Commandment signifies that love for God is reflected in love for humanity and willingness to preach the gospel of Jesus Christ to all (Matt. 22:36–40). If we love God, we will go to any length to reach people for Him. By contrast, our unwillingness to go and preach the good news indicates we do not love God as much as we say we do. Regardless of the timing of Christ's return, this is *the* eschatological challenge of history.

In the next two chapters, we will discuss how we can persevere through difficulty with proactive patience and grace. We will review a few constructive things we can do during difficult times to ease pain and to make the journey more meaningful.

Discussion Questions

1. What is your biggest fear about these difficult days before Christ's return?
2. How should the fact that no one is exempt from judgment motivate you to live more for eternal things?
3. What is your biggest challenge of obedience and faith in an uncertain future?

8

SELF-CARE:
THRIVING IN DIFFICULTY

Now if anyone builds on the foundation with gold, silver,
precious stones, wood, hay, straw—each one's work will
become manifest, for the Day will disclose it.

—PAUL (1 Corinthians 3:12–13)

Editor-in-Chief of *WORLD* magazine, Marvin Olasky, compares courage and perseverance in difficulty with cargo-laden ships that have "bottom." *Bottom* is an eighteenth-century mariner term for *ballast*, the stones or chunks of steel that were placed in a ship's hull to keep it low and steady during storms. Olasky says that having bottom is a necessity in today's morally ambiguous and politically tenuous environment: "It takes a lot of bottom to stand firm against" anti-Christian pressures in secular culture.[1]

The sad truth is we now battle on two fronts: our internal struggles and the external influences of culture. Both pressure us to abandon the moorings of faith, to cast off ballast, and sail recklessly into dangerous waters. Difficulty has a way of revealing our preparedness. It uncovers weaknesses, strips away the veneer of confidence, and reveals the substance of our core. We may think we are strong, but trouble always reveals the truth about strength. We may think we are prepared, but in a season of difficulty, what is down there in our core is the true indicator of our preparation and chances to survive a storm. If we have no "bottom," the struggle to stay afloat is far more tenuous.

As an indicator of human character, "bottom" is the foundational stuff—our relationship to God and His Word, and our covenantal/relational connections with His people—that carries us through life's inevitable ups and downs. In a storm, a ship's captain is more concerned about staying afloat than staying on course. The short-term urgency to secure the ship's integrity and ride out the tempest supersedes every other priority. But ships have sails too. When the seas are calm and winds are blowing favorably, sails propel a ship forward toward its destination. That we must haul them in during a storm, secure the lines, and batten down the hatches does not mean we abandoned our goals. After the storm passes, the sails are hoisted up the masts again. But if a ship sinks in a storm, the vision is lost. With that in mind, here are some ways we can practice self-care to prepare for, remain steady in, and even thrive during storms.

READ AND LEARN

The Bible is a great ballast-builder. It is a manual for life and success. But we must not turn to the Bible only in emergencies.

We must become familiar with the Bible *before* the storm and develop a habit of regular engagement with its contents. Bible reading is like studying a map or driving around in a new neighborhood. The more we get to know the area, the more we feel at home. The more we are at home, the better prepared we will be when difficulties come our way.

The Bible has authority and authenticity. It is "living and active" and resounds with truth on every page (Heb. 4:12). The Bible's truth is not abstract; it is real-life, relational truth that was revealed by God and lived by people who are connected with God. The Bible has relevance to our lives. A college student having difficulty with a fellow student or in finding the money to pay rent and tuition can find guidance, wisdom, and hope from the Bible's pages. A single mom, struggling to manage her time and budget and nurture little children, can discover a refuge in Scripture's comforting and instructive words. A young wife can find solace and courage in the pages of Scripture when her soldier husband is far away. A young man can discover wisdom from the Proverbs and the teachings of Paul about how to be a man of God and overcome youthful temptations. God's people find guidance in how to live and thrive in every human relationship—from marriage and the family to our conduct in the world with our neighbors and our roles in civil society.

When we dig deeper, we discover the Bible's historical accuracy. In other words, the Word of God relates to us—not as myth but as fact, not as philosophical conjecture but as truth, not as rambling ideas but as real wisdom revealed through the life and experiences of real people. The Bible connects us with a Person—in fact, the entire Bible is about a Person, the living God who has interacted with His beloved creation throughout history. The Bible is a personal message from the One who knows us intimately and wants us to know Him and His dealings with His creation.

Over one hundred years ago, William Evans wrote, "There is probably no greater need in the Christian Church today than that its membership should be made acquainted with the fundamental facts and doctrines of the Christian faith."[2] For a follower of Jesus Christ, engagement with Scripture is a primary source for spiritual strength and growth. It provides guidance, gives comfort, and offers reassurance through the ups and downs of life. It feeds our souls. In truth, we meet Jesus in the Bible, not only as a historical figure, but as God's living Word (see John 1:1, 14; Heb. 1:1–2) revealed to us by the Holy Spirit. There simply is no substitute for the personal nurture that comes from interaction with Scripture.

I remember a time when our family was struggling financially. We were home from the mission field, the four of us living with my wife's parents in their two-bedroom, one-bathroom house. One morning, I was studying in the basement, where I had set up a small card table and folding chair under a dangling light bulb. Surrounded by tools, stacked boxes, and gray concrete walls covered with shelves of canned goods from their garden, I put my head in my hands, and my elbows on that dusty card table, and prayed. I opened my Bible, pleading in my heart, "Lord, we can't continue like this. This meager support isn't working. We need Your help! I don't know what to do. Please show me what to do!" I somehow turned to John 14, and Jesus' words leaped out:

> "Let not your hearts be troubled. Believe in God; believe also in me. In my Father's house are many rooms. If it were not so, would I have told you that I go to prepare a place for you? And if I go and prepare a place for you, I will come again and will take you to myself, that where I am you may be also." (John 14:1–3)

Jesus was speaking to His disciples about His imminent death and what would follow. I knew this. I had memorized this Scripture as a young boy. But in this moment, Jesus' words took on new meaning for me and challenged me to see Him, not as indifferent and aloof, but as near, comforting, and pro-active. In my mind, I saw Jesus and heaven's hosts preparing something yet unseen for our family. This fresh insight became a driving message in my life in the coming season, a message I preached: "We often think of heaven as an inactive place," I said, "where God is seated on the throne and Jesus is by His side . . . but in fact heaven is filled with activity. When Jesus left the disciples at Calvary, He was active, 'preparing a place' for them! In the same way, we must see God's apparent absence not as abandonment, but as active preparation of something new for us." After that pleading prayer in a dingy basement, God began to bring change to our little family's future and our financial situation. Things did not change overnight, but my courage was boosted with a renewed belief in God's nearness and favor even in difficulty. The insight was transforming!

There is a miraculous component to Bible reading; we should read it prayerfully, reverently, and with an expectation that God will speak to us through its pages. The Bible is filled with relevant history, amazing promises, powerful doctrines, profound revelations about God's identity and work, sobering predictions about the future of this planet, and clear assessments about humanity's condition. God's Word has answers! But those answers are not casually acquired. We discover God's treasures when we fervently search for them by diligently seeking Him.

> My son, if you receive my words
>   and treasure up my commandments with you,
> making your ear attentive to wisdom
>   and inclining your heart to understanding;
> yes, if you call out for insight
>   and raise your voice for understanding,
> if you seek it like silver
>   and search for it as for hidden treasures,
> then you will understand the fear of the Lord
>   and find the knowledge of God. (Prov. 2:1–5)

We should also read Christian literature and listen to Bible-centered preachers, teachers, theologians, philosophers, and writers. They help guide our learning and our search for answers to our questions. Biblical teachers offer insights we might never get on our own. But when we are casual about the things of God, we become vulnerable to whatever is the most tantalizing image and attractive voice around us. Gordon MacDonald says such a mind

> too easily accepts a blanket ideology that offers a "correct" response for everything. . . . The disciplined, trained mind, however. . . . weighs every question and asks if Scripture speaks directly or indirectly to the matter. It weighs it in the light of history. . . . It measures the matter in terms of its ability to reflect the redeeming love of God.[3]

By asking us to diligently seek Him, God is not toying with us, nor is He hiding from us. He is simply asking us to be serious about a serious matter. Think about it this way: no employer ever hired someone who showed up late for the interview, submitted an incomplete application, and yawned during the process. No coach ever put a player into the game who habitually daydreamed during practice and slept through debriefings. In the same way, God is looking for hunger and diligence when we come to Him. Not because He needs it, but because we do. There is no faking it with God! God "rewards those who earnestly seek him" (Heb. 11:6 NIV). When we diligently and patiently seek God, even in times of longsuffering, God will respond.

WORSHIP

If reading engages the mind, then worship engages the soul. When we open our hearts to God and give Him access to the deepest parts of our being—our fears, our sins, our frustrations, and our need for love, understanding, and guidance—and turn to Him in faith and hope in His promises and acknowledge Him for who He is, even when we do not understand every detail, our surrender and confession is worship in God's ears. And such worship has a transforming effect on our hearts. Why? Because it connects us at the heart level with God. Worship has a strong intuitive component, but it begins with a decision. We turn to God intentionally with our heart, expressing our needs to Him in faith, honoring Him for who He is. Worship is also our gratitude, expressed to God, remembering what He has done for us. It is an exercise of faith and hope and a refusal to turn away from Him in despair.

Reading the Bible grounds our thinking in truth about the living God. Worship connects our hearts to Him. The first is more cognitive, the second more emotive. The one seeks objective understanding; the other seeks intuitive connection. There is some danger in categorizing Scripture reading and worship in this way. We do it here only to make a point. In both Scripture reading and worship we seek God, to learn from Him, to grow in Him, and to connect with Him in both our minds and our hearts. Scripture reading and worship also have individual and corporate components. We study the Bible in solitude; we learn together in our community of faith. We worship God when we are alone and when we gather with others.

The emotive, intuitive, "right brain" feature of worship defies logic and reasoning.[4] By simple surrender, we worship God. As Paul said, we worship with both our mind and our spirit (1 Cor. 14:15). We do not abandon reason, and yet our experience with worship can transcend reason. Eugene Peterson explains the mind/heart paradox of worship:

> We think that if we don't *feel* something there can be no authenticity in *doing* it. But the wisdom of God says something different: that we can *act* ourselves into a new way of feeling much quicker than we can *feel* ourselves into a new way of acting. Worship is an *act* that develops feelings for God, not a *feeling* for God that is expressed in an act of worship.[5]

The book of Psalms is a human expression paragon: awe, happiness, contentment, rejoicing, worship, weeping, anger, bitterness, contempt, depression, fear. The Psalms was *the* hymn book for an entire nation. Today, Christians recite and sometimes sing the Psalms in public worship services; at home we find solace and comfort in the verses of these ancient poems. The stunning imagery of Psalm 23 is an exemplar of the book's beauty and poignancy. One is overwhelmed with almost every read:

> The LORD is my shepherd; I shall not want.
>   He makes me lie down in green pastures.
> He leads me beside still waters.
>   He restores my soul.
> He leads me in paths of righteousness
>   for his name's sake.

Even though I walk through the valley of the shadow
   of death,
   I will fear no evil,
for you are with me;
   your rod and your staff,
   they comfort me. (Ps. 23:1–4)

But not every psalm is happy. Some, like Psalm 137, may be appropriate only in times of great difficulty, when God's people, both publicly and privately, express their grief through deep lamentations.

By the waters of Babylon,
   there we sat down and wept,
   when we remembered Zion. . . .
O daughter of Babylon, doomed to be destroyed,
   blessed shall he be who repays you
   with what you have done to us!
Blessed shall he be who takes your little ones
   and dashes them against the rock!
(Ps. 137:1, 8–9)

Paul Carter asks, "Does this verse really belong in scripture?"[6] He then explains when we understand what the Jewish people endured during the Babylonian siege of Jerusalem in 586 BC—"Wives were raped, children were trampled, families were ruined and lives torn apart"[7]—we can understand why a psalm like this was written. In their anguish the Jews had no other poetry to write; they had only lament. God permitted them to express their sorrow and grief in prayer. He preserved those prayers for us to read and commiserate. Carter explains the context brilliantly:

> We live in peaceful times. Our grandparents who fought in WW2 and who lived the reality of the Holocaust can likely relate to this verse much better than we can. . . . we must be careful to react to the words that *are there* and not to the words *that we imagine are there*. . . . the Psalmist doesn't say: "How happy I will be when I smash some Babylonian babies against the wall!" . . .
>
> He says: "Blessed is HE who repays you. Who does to you what you did to us."[8]

Sometimes all that people have left is grief. Christians, more than any other people on the planet, can lament with people who are experiencing sorrow. We can't fix such problems. They are too big for us. But we can come alongside of those who suffer. This is what Jesus does for us. By the Holy Spirit, He comes to our side in comfort. We can do the same for others, bringing the presence of Jesus with us. We can pray, befriend, lend a hand, offer a gentle presence, and in time lead people to the healing that comes from the One who has healed us.

> Blessed be the God and Father of our Lord Jesus Christ, the Father of mercies and God of all comfort, who comforts us in all our affliction, so that we may be able to comfort those who are in any affliction, with the comfort

with which we ourselves are comforted by God. For as we share abundantly in Christ's sufferings, so through Christ we share abundantly in comfort too. (2 Cor. 1:3–5)

Author Andrea Palpant Dilley shares how personal angst and disappointment first led her away from faith in God and then back to Him again:

> When people ask me what drove me out the doors of the church and then what brought me back, my answer to both questions is the same. I left the church in part because I was mad at God about human suffering and injustice. And I came back to church because of that same struggle.[9]

Dilley discovered that talk about justice only makes sense when we view it from the framework of an "objective morality."[10] And objective morality can only be understood from a God-oriented framework. Without God, there is no objective morality "out there." There are no absolutes, no outside framework of right and wrong; we can therefore do and believe whatever we want.

Christians believe God is there, and He is just and will work for justice even when we don't feel Him or understand what He is doing. In difficult times, we do internal work by expressing our angst to God. This pouring out of our hearts to God, even as bewilderment and pain, is worship! Worship bolsters our faith in part because, in the expression of our hearts, we surrender to Someone who is bigger, stronger, and wiser than ourselves. Failure to do this internal work, to humble ourselves and surrender, almost always results in a form of internal and external disintegration when angst comes out in self-destructive forms. For the hurting soul, the book of Psalms is perhaps one of the most powerful and consoling books of the Bible. The worship and devotional connections with God in these sacred poems reflects every emotion known to man. It is in these words we find solace while we wait for God's deliverance and answers.

CREATE

Psychologist and author Mihaly Csikszentmihalyi suggests that creativity, where people experiment with "new ways for baking stuffed artichokes, or original ways of decorating the living room for a party," is healthy for the soul.[11] It enriches our lives, provides a form of diversion, connects us with other like-minded people, and counters unhealthy impulses during times of difficulty. God's creative handiwork in the human design shows how "fearfully and wonderfully made" we all are (Ps. 139:14). We are both analytical and imaginative. We are both logical and intuitive. We think and we feel. We observe and we are aware of our ability to observe. We analyze and we dream. We sometimes feel euphoric; at other times, we are sad.

What exactly is creativity, and where does it come from? God's creation of human beings in His image can be inferred to include human creativity. We can't create as God did— forming substance from nothing—but we can create using the materials of the created world. Our minds continually have new ideas. We express creative inclinations with our hands by building, designing, or playing. We write, we sing, we dance. We see, hear, and feel creatively, envisioning things that do not yet exist. In joy and in sorrow, creativity pours out of us. Humankind's fall into sin did not nullify this unique quality; it only defiled creativity into corrupt expressions like idolatry, lust, and greed.

When we live outside of God's redemption, our fallen nature is vulnerable to destructive influences and appetites. We hurt ourselves and people around us. But when we allow God's redemption to work in us, even in difficulty we can find refuge in healthy expressions of our pain and grief through prayer, worship, *and* creativity.

I remember when my wife and I were going through some very personal difficulties, I came face-to-face with choices about how I would handle my pain and loneliness. I could express my angst in unhealthy ways that would lead to destruction, or I could find creative expression that would be healthy to my soul. So, I picked up my guitar and began writing songs. I experimented with poetry. I wrote a book. My son and I entered an acting troupe in our city and joined the cast of a Christmas play. For physical health, I started riding a bicycle. I learned how to surf.

All the while, my wife and I sought counsel and worked on our issues and our marriage. The end result of that difficult road was that we grew and our marriage was restored; we learned how to communicate better, to be more skilled at kindness and thoughtfulness. We learned how to lean on each other and attend to each other's needs. We learned to like then love each other again, all of which led us to rediscover marriage intimacy. In the interim period, while we worked on the issues, when we had to persevere, we found healthy ways to deal with our pain. Both of us had to avoid destructive behavior that could have done permanent damage to our family. Our saving grace was Jesus and our commitment to Him, and a refusal to consider divorce. We were determined to press through. In those times I found great solace in creative expression. Creativity was a healthy and cathartic activity in the waiting period.

During that season, I started a club called the Christian Artist's Guild in our church. We invited musicians, vocalists, painters, sculptors, writers, poets, actors, and more to attend. At the start of every meeting, I shared a creative devotion from Scripture or a book. Then, we transitioned to an "open mic" period where anyone could share their creative work for three minutes. We had only one rule: no pornography or blasphemy. Anger was okay. Sadness was okay. Comedy and sarcasm were fine too. Authenticity was expected. I sometimes taught from the Psalms, sharing the strong emotions—both negative and positive—that fill this book of the Bible, explaining that God is not surprised or offended by our pain or anguish. When we pour out our souls authentically to Him, He welcomes our creative expression as a form of affirmative honor of Him in our lives. The Guild was a huge success in our community and encouraged many fledgling artists to take a risk by sharing their talents and work with others.

DIVERT FROM SIN TO GOD

The book of Genesis records God's pleasure in creation.[12] It certainly was a delight for humanity too (see Gen. 3:1–7). Eden was a biological and geographical miracle. Adam and Eve lived in a utopian paradise with God as a constant companion. Eden was filled with things to do. Some have suggested that work came after the fall, pointing to references about cursed ground, weeds, and the "sweat of your face" (Gen. 3:17–19). These conditions certainly indicate that, after the fall, life decayed and work became more tedious. Philip Graham Ryken suggests that the rhythm of work and rest was God's design from the beginning, ordained by God *before* the fall (Gen. 2:15). Had we not turned away from God, both work and rest would have been equally fulfilling.

> Work is a divine gift that goes back before the Fall, when "The LORD God took the man and put him in the Garden of Eden to work it and keep it" (Genesis 2:15). We were made for work. The trouble is that our work has been cursed by sin. . . . But it was not this way from the beginning.[13]

I tend to agree with Ryken's position. Sin robbed us of the ability to enjoy life, both in work and play. Shame, guilt, and separation from our Creator stole something from us. That work became more tedious, that death entered the picture, that shame and guilt became a part of the human experience, that greed and jealousy and lust created conflict between human beings, beginning with Cain and Abel, all illustrate the fact that we lost our peace with God and our ability to enjoy life as He intended. We lost our purity, we lost our way, and we lost a relationship with God Himself! Now we live outside of Eden, where sin contaminates and corrodes everything.

Western culture's advancements haven't solved our problems. We have leisure time, but its soul is often missing. Richard Winter suggests that a disquieting feature of modern society is boredom. We have everything we need and want, but it still isn't enough. He cites a 2001 PBS documentary called *Frontier House* that tracked three California families who adopted lifestyles of 1800s frontier families for six months in Montana. They built houses, planted food, tended livestock, and caught fish in the stream. After their return to Malibu, "one of the children was having a hard time adjusting to a life where basic needs are met so much more easily. She said, 'Life in 2000 is boring. Where's the fun in going to the mall every day?'"[14] Winter quotes William May to further his point:

> Far more serious . . . is the condition of the man who
> is melancholic and dejected in the very presence of the
> good. Such a man has his son, but his son bores him. He
> possesses his beloved, but finds her incapable of stirring
> his interest. He has been promised the presence of God,
> but this promise leaves him cold. To such a man the
> presence or absence of the good makes no difference. His
> desire for the good is dead. . . . *Perhaps boredom is the best
> modern term to characterize this deadness of soul.*[15]

We in Western culture must now face the unpleasant fact that nothing really makes us happy anymore. We have everything we want, but contentment eludes us. In truth, this is a problem of all humanity. We in Western culture should understand this more keenly, simply because we have more of everything. We have been able to try everything, buy everything, and go everywhere. Yet we are still not happy and we still cannot get along with each other. Perhaps happiness and healthy living is based in something else, in an internal experience, where we connect with God in simplicity and rediscover Him. The salvation of Jesus Christ not only secures our place in eternity; it also empowers us to live wholesome lives and healthy relationships in the here and now.

What Does It Mean to Divert?

Sin is the crux of the matter and has a way of ruining everything. A good vacation can go sour if one person in the family becomes irritable and uncooperative. One bad member can demoralize an entire team, at work or on the sports field. To divert does not mean to pursue external stimuli just for the purpose of a change of pace. It means to recognize my propensity toward ruin and *make an intentional decision to reconnect with God*, the source of real meaning and happiness, especially in difficult circumstances. I divert from my human inclinations and turn back to God. I seek His wisdom and purposes. I look to Him for joy, when joy cannot be found anywhere else.

Divert also means to stop. To turn around. To go another way. To divert is to repent. Stop doing destructive things and entertaining destructive thoughts and attitudes. Turn. Divert from sin. When I divert, I lean into the Holy Spirit, ask God for help, walk in Him, and allow the Holy Spirit to fill in the empty places in my soul and begin producing His spiritual fruit.

Diversions, like a weekend at the beach or a hiking trip in the mountains, are great, but we must always remember, even the garden of Eden was nothing more than a jungle without the presence of God. A dream job can become a nightmare when our soul is in disarray. The same is true in marriage. A happily compatible couple, who were once in love, can suddenly turn on each other when one or both allow the pressures of life, or sinful inclinations or habits, to corrode the relationship.

Especially in difficulty, ask God to make you hungry for Him again. Take a quieter walk, along a longer path up a steeper slope to a higher place. Determine to seek Him until He is found. Turn from sin. Place Jesus at the center of everything and ask Him to join you in every detail of your life. Look your challenges squarely in the face and refuse to allow them to get the best of you. Divert. Turn your heart toward God. In our noisy culture that clamors for our attention, and with our propensity to blindly think more highly of ourselves than we should, and to minimize our sinful nature, this can be difficult, but, in the end, it will pay eternal dividends!

Difficulty is actually a gift that removes the temporal things we cling to. Difficulty reminds us to reach for something of deeper and more enduring value. The time we spend in perseverance through difficulty can teach us these vital truths until they become habits. To find simple solace and contentment in God, to be wrapped in His goodness and peace, to let go of unhealthy things, and to reach beyond ourselves and the distractions of life, and take hold of God.

LIVE FAITHFULLY

Faithful living integrates all that we have talked about in this chapter. A pastor friend once commented to me about faithfulness to his marriage. "I do the math when I'm tempted to wander," he said. "When you add it all up, faithfulness just makes more sense." Faithful living grows from our love for God, but it is more than an emotional response to God and His ways. Faith is a choice to trust God, which is followed by action. By a decision to trust God, we ascribe *worth* to Him, and declare that He is worth following, and He is worth our surrendered allegiance. In short, when we have learned that following Jesus and living His way just makes sense, we have "done the math."

God is worthy of both our affections and our obedience. We worship God when we lean on Him. When we live faithfully, by our alignment with His character and surrender to His rule, we ascribe worth to God and honor Him. In faithful living, we allow God to influence more than our inner lives and feelings. We welcome Him to guide our behavior. It is in faithful living that our inner person and our outer life integrate into real discipleship as a follower of Jesus.

I vividly remember my grandmother pointing out to me the reasonableness of faithful living. I was hardly ten years old. She had a loving and direct way of helping me learn. My maternal grandparents were dairy farmers. Rain or shine, hot or cold, sick or healthy, a farmer rises early every morning to milk the cows. I loved going to my grandparents' farm—helping with the chores, climbing around in the hayloft, feeding the chickens—but for an adolescent boy, getting out of bed at 5:00 a.m. wasn't a part of the enjoyment. "The cows don't care how you feel," my grandmother said, prodding me one early morning while I resisted getting out of bed. "They need to be milked, so up and at 'em!"

Faithful living validates our feelings but subordinates them to our responsibilities. Faithful people "make the world go 'round." They deliver our mail, pick up our garbage, and keep water flowing from our faucets. We sleep well at night because police officers cruise our neighborhoods, and the military watches over our national security. We hope these people are happy, but we also know that happiness isn't the essence of their service or responsibility. We expect and appreciate their faithful attention to their jobs regardless of what is going on in their personal lives. Faithful living makes life tolerable and sensible for everyone! Faithfulness is love in action. This is the essence of Jesus Christ's obedience at Calvary. It wasn't easy, but Jesus laid down His life on the cross because it needed to be done. Like Jesus, as His followers, we have God and His infinite resources to back us up and empower us to live this way.

While Paul was incarcerated in Rome, he chose to overcome the desperate conditions of prison. Rather than languish in self-pity, he found a way to live faithfully by leaning into the abiding grace and love of God. He prayed for people and wrote letters of encouragement and instruction to them.

He worshiped God, read the Scriptures, and discovered truth about Jesus and shared them with God's people. We are still reading Paul's letters two thousand years later! We should never insist on personal happiness at the expense of faithful living. It is inherently self-defeating. God Himself stands with us in the difficulty, ready to encourage and empower us.

At the heart of faithful living is Jesus Christ. We live and serve and survive because we love Jesus. Our love for Him constrains us and keeps us on the tracks. The world might be disintegrating all around us, but the courageous soul seeks God and His faithfulness. In hardship, I can turn my back on God and let my life erode into self-destruction. Or I can lean into Jesus Christ while consciously practicing these five elements of self-care.

Discussion Questions

1. What Scripture do you turn to frequently for consolation and encouragement? How is it helpful to you in worship?
2. Do you have an expression of creativity that provides you rest and inspiration, and how has this helped you in times of difficulty and been a blessing and encouragement to others?
3. How can you eliminate unhealthy distractions and seek God more meaningfully?
4. In what ways are you intentionally living faithfully?

9

PERSEVERANCE AS A LIFESTYLE

"I live in my current reality . . . I don't
believe God is holding out on me."

—DAVID MAYO

Have you ever thought about why you like some stories more than others? Why some books and movies are just *better*? Something about the story—the characters or the plot—draws you in and keeps you reading or watching. It's almost magical. We love to get lost in a great story! In a character-driven story, the hero is usually introduced immediately. The reader or viewer must quickly bond with the hero or she will lose interest. A good writer makes the hero interesting and likeable: he has emotions, he's quirky, he has flaws and vulnerabilities, all of which makes us identify with him and like him. To make a hero likeable, writers use a trick called "saving the cat."[1]

In the movie *Rocky Balboa*,[2] Rocky is a retired professional boxer. One night, he drives a single mother and her teenage son home after an evening shift at his restaurant. "Why are you being so nice?" the woman asks suspiciously. Rocky defends himself: "Why does there have to be a reason for being nice?" He walks up to the house's dark porch, reaches into his pocket, and pulls out a light bulb. The porch light is burned out—he had noticed this earlier—so he brought a new bulb to change it. He removes the old bulb, screws in the new one, and presto! The porch floods with light. Rocky Balboa just "saved the cat!" When Rocky changes that light bulb, we like him immediately.

Author Don Miller says we should live our lives like Rocky Balboa and make our story worth watching.[3] In essence, Miller says we should make our lives, our story, the best it can be. As a follower of Jesus, we take this seriously. God is watching. Our intimacy with Jesus, our respect for God's ways, and Christ's love for humanity, affects us all the time. These things continually guide our behavior in the little things so that the pattern of our life in the aggregate becomes a story that honors God and is worth sharing with others.

Like all human beings, we have quirks and flaws too. We make mistakes, but we "save a cat" sometimes. We try to be amicable and trustworthy. When we face a challenge, we engage it courageously and fight the battle with endurance. We are fair and just and kind to people around us. We keep our promises. We take hits, we fall down, but we get back up again. And we never, ever quit. In the end, when our story is wrapping up, we have learned something. We grew and we lived for the glory of God, both through the good times and with patient perseverance in difficulty.

We like watching good stories; living them is a lot harder.

Perseverance is tough! But this is the kind of person God asks us to be. As Christians, we persevere through difficulty, not for ourselves, but for the glory of God, and so that other people can see Him in us. When we live a life of perseverance, our story becomes one worth telling, worth following, worth remembering. Our life can be remembered as a legacy rather than a tragedy. Why? Because it reflects a quality of God that supersedes selfish human interests and ambitions and points to the One whose purposes are higher and better. To put it in biblical terms, the heroic, well-lived life of a Christ follower reflects the grace and goodness of God.

BEAUTY AS CHARACTER

Tim Keller tells the story about taking a music appreciation class when he was in college:

> My professor liked Mozart, so I listened to a lot of Mozart in order to get an A, in order to get good grades, in order to graduate with honors, in order to get a good job, in order to make money. So, I listened to Mozart to make money. But, today, if you know me, you know I spend a lot of money to listen to Mozart. Why? It doesn't get me anything now, does it? Why do I like listening to Mozart? It's beautiful. . . . It's a satisfying thing in itself.[4]

Keller says Christians live the same way—from an inner quality he calls beauty. When our lives reflect beauty, our works of service and our acts of goodness and justice are not our own.

They reflect Jesus Christ, who gave us His beauty. We don't "listen to Mozart"—reflecting Christ's beauty through our lives—because we have to. We listen because we want to. Perseverance is the fruit of something! We persevere because we have experienced the goodness and kindness of God. If we live and thrive through life's wonder and tragedy, that glorious, complex fabric and its sometimes painful unraveling, we do it because Jesus Christ is beautiful even when life hurts. We pursue His beauty, our lives reflect His beauty, and we share it with others for no greater reason than we want to. We want to because of an overflowing appreciation for what Jesus has done for us.

The apostle Paul wrote two letters to Timothy, his spiritual son. Timothy was an emerging Christian leader living in the wealthy and influential Roman port city of Ephesus. He was gifted and committed to Jesus, but like all young men, he struggled with weaknesses and insecurities. He carried the added pressure of pastoring a large church full of broken people. Paul is gracious to Timothy always, but he also upholds God's promises, commands, and expectations. And Paul never lets Timothy off the hook. In the first letter, Paul writes:

> Don't let anyone look down on you because you are young, but set an example for the believers. . . . Until I come, devote yourself to the public reading of Scripture. . . . Do not neglect your gift. . . .
>
> Be diligent in these matters; give yourself wholly to them. . . . Watch your life and doctrine closely. Persevere in them, because if you do, you will save both yourself and your hearers. (1 Tim. 4:12–16 NIV)

Paul's words contain a litany of lifestyle bearings and behaviors that apply to every Christian. Commenting on these verses, Gordon MacDonald says, "Paul is challenging Timothy to scour his life, to place it—as it were—under a microscope and assure that every part of it is operating according to the highest Christian standards."[5] This "scouring" of our life for problems and weaknesses is not an easy or intuitive task. Much of life requires our wholehearted attention and takes more work than we want to invest. Such is the challenge of every bad habit, every self-indulgent behavior, and everything we glibly ignore.

Why do we need to deal with this stuff? In short, because flaws kill beauty. As Christians, our flaws are not who we are, at least not the way God sees us. We deal with them because sin can turn a beautiful thing into ugliness, a hero into a has-been. If they are ignored, sinful behavior will sidetrack our lives and short-circuit God's purposes. We do much better when we confront our brokenness head-on rather than avoid and deny it. Scripture gets to the issue of human depravity at the very beginning[6] and stays with it to the last chapter of the Bible (see Rev. 22:3, 11, 15). The apostle Paul affirms this ancient theme: "As it is written: 'None is righteous, no, not one; no one understands; no one seeks for God. All have turned aside; together they have become worthless; no one does good, not even one'" (Rom. 3:10–12).

Jesus intimated the same when He called Israel to repent and when He reminded a rich young ruler that there is no good person, only God.[7] God is not being unkind by pointing out our sinfulness. Christians view the hard truth about sin through the lens of God's benevolence. He speaks this truth to us in love.

Even secular culture understands the principle of truth-telling. A baseball coach tells a player *what he is doing wrong.* He points out what must be done to improve performance. The player might be frustrated, but when he listens and invests effort, his skill improves. A college professor grades papers, *marking wrong answers* with red ink. The student might feel bad about a low grade, but hurting the student's feelings isn't the professor's goal. The student's proficiency is. Recovering alcoholics know the first step to sobriety is brutal honesty. Until an addict says, "I'm an alcoholic. I need help," nothing will change. At some point in our lives, we all need brutal honesty. We all have issues that, if unchecked, will consume us. Paul's confession, "I know that nothing good dwells in me," was a personal assessment of his life without Jesus Christ (Rom. 7:18). As a Christian, Paul lived his life with its reality:

> [Jesus] finally presented himself alive to me. It was fitting that I bring up the rear. I don't deserve to be included . . . having spent all those early years trying my best to stamp God's church right out of existence. But because God was so gracious, so very generous, here I am. (1 Cor. 15:8–10 MSG)

Paul lived with gratitude and humility for what Christ did for him, and never forgot who he was before he met Jesus. The transformation turned him into a tenacious follower.

And I'm not about to let his grace go to waste. Haven't I worked hard trying to do more than any of the others? Even then, my work didn't amount to all that much. It was God giving me the work to do, God giving me the energy to do it. (1 Cor. 15:10–11 MSG)

PREPARATION FOR CHALLENGES

As Christians, we struggle against our baser appetites and the influences of the culture in which we live. We trust God while being realistic about the journey of faith and obedience we must walk. Jesus' redemption was not cheaply won; it will not be easily realized. Though we are secure in our relationship with Him, we must "work out our own salvation with fear and trembling" (Phil. 2:12). There are challenges on every side. Tim Keller emphasizes the key role of difficult experiences in our walk toward Christian growth and sanctification:

Suffering is actually at the heart of the Christian story. Suffering is the result of our turn away from God, and therefore it was the way through which God himself in Jesus Christ came and rescued us for himself. And now it is how we suffer that comprises one of the main ways we become great and Christ-like, holy and happy, and a crucial way we show the world the love and glory of our Savior.[8]

We *should* be fearful on this long road to Christlikeness. A healthy fear alerts us to danger and reminds us about our limits and vulnerabilities. We do not fear God's disapproval, but we should fear our inclinations. God's mercies are new every morning but so are our appetites (see Lam. 3:22–23)! "I discipline my body," Paul says, "and bring it under control, lest after preaching to others I myself should be disqualified" (1 Cor. 9:27).

This great confluence of bold forward vision and somber caution, of looking confidently ahead while measuring reality with caution, is the mark of Christian maturity. A lack of boldness means we won't take risks. A lack of preparation means we will fail along the way. There is a delicate balance between bold vision and cautious preparation.

In 1914, British explorer Ernest Shackleton boarded the ship *Endurance* with his crew of twenty-seven men and sailed to the South Atlantic to claim the status as the first person to cross the Antarctic continent on foot. When they reached their destination in the Weddell Sea, less than ninety miles to their destination, the *Endurance* became trapped in ice and was soon crushed. Shackleton and his crew were stranded for twenty months before they were rescued.[9]

This was not Shackleton's first attempt to conquer the freezing continent. Thirteen years earlier, in 1901, he had accompanied Captain Robert Falcon Scott on the ship *Discovery* to "reach the as yet unclaimed South Pole and win it for Britain."[10] When they reached McMurdo Sound, Captain Scott chose two men (one was Shackleton) to accompany him—along with nineteen dogs and five loaded sleds—to make the treacherous 1,600-mile walking and skiing round trip to the pole "through an entirely unknown and uncharted environment."[11] They endured starvation, scurvy, and the death of their dogs, which they butchered one by one to stay alive. The party got within 745 miles north of the pole before turning back in defeat. Documentarian Caroline Alexander comments,

> This first Antarctic trek established the pattern of heroic suffering that would characterize British expeditions. Yet even a casual perusal of the explorers' diaries suggests *this suffering was unnecessary.* . . .
>
> . . . Scott and his companions had not taken the time to become proficient on skis, nor did they have any knowledge of driving dogs. Their prodigious difficulties, therefore, were the result of almost inconceivable incompetence, not necessity. And the men were starving—not because unforeseen disaster had taken their supplies, but because they had not rationed sufficient food.[12]

What can be learned from the failings of these brave adventurers? First, we are naïve to think our journey will be free of difficulty and that we will always know what we are doing. It will not be easy, there will be difficulties, and *we do not know* what we are doing! We admire Scott's and Shackleton's courage. We could learn from their overconfidence. Their failure to properly prepare teaches us much about the human tendency to overestimate our abilities and underestimate our limits and vulnerabilities.

COMING TO TERMS WITH OUR LIMITS

I recently had breakfast with my friend David Mayo. David is a fifty-something professional with a ruddy, outdoorsy physique, a head of wavy salt-and-pepper hair, and an immensely engaging countenance that shines through the twinkle in his eyes and an inexorable positive attitude. David manages a Christian television station. The media exposure makes him a bit of a celebrity in our area. It isn't uncommon for him to run into friends and fans when he is out and about, which happened at the IHOP restaurant where we met. He unfailingly treats everyone like he or she is his best friend.

David and his wife, Beverly, are active in the community too—in philanthropic causes, in local cycling, running, and swimming events, in church, and even in politics. David swims better, cycles faster, and generally outdoes me in everything, a fact that has never mattered to either of us. The competition, if one could call it that, gives us stuff to do and talk about together. I admire David Mayo and am honored to be his friend.

There is only one difference between David and me: he sits down for everything he does. David has been in a wheelchair since he was a teenager. Many years ago, on a hot July summer afternoon, when his family was vacationing in Idaho, fifteen-year-old David left camp and set out alone for some rock climbing. When he was thirty-five feet up a cliff wall, he fell. The fall broke his back, severed his spinal cord, and left David lying in a rocky crag unable to move until his family found him several hours later.

After helicopter transport to a nearby Emergency Room, and nine hours in surgery to fuse three vertebrae in his spine, David spent the next sixty days recovering in two hospitals. When he was released, David expected that by Christmas he would be walking again. That was forty years ago. With his hopes of walking again dashed over and over, young David suffered through a long and grueling ordeal of recovery and grief, an excruciating journey to accept a new reality. To learn how to get around without the use of his legs. To learn the tricky balance between autonomy and dependence. And to deal with the new and very personal limits in his anatomy. David battled demons of anger, bitterness, and all the conflicting emotions one would expect from such a tremendous loss for a young man.

David eventually came to terms with his condition. Now David lives his story courageously and admirably. He told me over our breakfast that he still holds to the belief that all things are possible with God (Matt. 19:26). He daily looks for God's miracle-working power in his life, while, in the interim, "I live in my current reality." With his usual optimism, David added, "I don't believe God is holding out on me." As we wrapped up breakfast, David shared something he learned from the apostle Paul:

> As servants of God we commend ourselves in every way: by great endurance, in afflictions, hardships, calamities, beatings, imprisonments, riots, labors, sleepless nights, hunger; by purity, knowledge, patience, kindness, the Holy Spirit, genuine love; by truthful speech,

and the power of God; with the weapons of righteousness for the right hand and for the left. (2 Cor. 6:4–7)

"The first half of this text," David explained, "was the stuff
Paul had to endure: afflictions, hardships, and so forth. The
second half—purity, knowledge, patience, kindness, and the
Holy Spirit—was the *way* he did it." David would know. Forty
years in a wheelchair will teach a lot if one is willing to learn.

All of us must come to terms with our aspirations and
our limits, and make decisions about how we will live on this
bumpy road called life. Will we be bitter, or will we thrive?
Will we hold God responsible for our difficulties, or will we
rise above them and persevere by allowing the Holy Spirit to
fill us with patience, kindness, and faith despite our circumstances? Will we succumb to self-pity? Will we shift the blame
on others? Will we run away in rebellion? Or will we cooperate
with God in overcoming our pain and trust Him to complete
His purposes in our lives? Can we be okay with some things
inadequate, imperfect, and unresolved? Can we ask for help
when we need it?

David has learned all of these things. He has learned
them so well that now life is a joyous, imperfect adventure.
I'm learning a lot from guys like the apostle Paul and my
friend David. They teach me about human brokenness and
even more about God's powerful redemption. Bad stuff happens, people are mean, we make mistakes, we suffer, and the
world is just terribly broken. The only way out of this mess
is God's redemption in Jesus Christ, a plan started with utter
humility and concluded with death and resurrection. We

walk—sometimes with joy, sometimes with sorrow—but always with faith and perseverance, trusting our lives to the One who gave His life so we could receive forgiveness and salvation from Him.

What if, like Paul and Jesus, we could see our suffering in light of resurrection? *Every difficulty* is an opportunity to become like Jesus in death so we can be like Him in resurrection. Paul reminded the Corinthians, "I die every day" (1 Cor. 15:31). Paul figured it out and offered himself over and over to life or death for Jesus' sake. For the Christian, Paul knew, death is never final. Resurrection always follows. "Oh death, where is your victory?" he declared. "Oh death, where is your sting?" he declared again (1 Cor. 15:55–56). Jesus is risen. We too shall be raised. There is no sting in death. This is our living hope! For every Christian, there is therefore no despair, but only hope in the glorious overcoming power of God put on display in history, and also in a promised future, through the finished work of our Lord and Savior Jesus Christ!

Discussion Questions

1. What might be holding you back from living a more compelling story?
2. How does repentance and beauty help you push through difficulty, face fear, overcome an obstacle, or patiently persevere?
3. What limitations do you have and how have those humbled you and drawn you to Christ?

EPILOGUE

Senator Ben Sasse says that "loneliness is killing us."[1] Among other things, he cites the skyrocketing rates of suicide and drug overdose deaths in America. In 2016, forty-five thousand Americans took their lives; two years earlier, nearly sixty-five thousand died from drug overdoses.[2] We live in one of the most prosperous nations in the world, the proverbial land of opportunity, but we fail again and again to find happiness. Sasse worries that too many don't have what he describes as a "thick" community, where people know and look out for one another and are invested in enduring relationships.[3]

It's hard to make a biblical case for perseverance without including the framework of the nuclear family. Ironically, the opposite is true in Western culture: it's difficult to make a cultural case for perseverance in the Western worldview by *including* the nuclear family. We are wired for individualism. Our worldview is founded on the presupposition that if I achieve anything in life it is because I exerted individual effort. I pulled myself up by my bootstraps; I did it on my own; I made my own road; I turned my back on opposition and refused to let anything or anyone stand in my way. Sadly, our Christian view of salvation reflects this individualistic paradigm, and we focus on Scriptures that support the bias. Invitations to receive Christ in a public event are predicated, "Every eye closed and no one looking around," while the preacher encourages individuals to do personal business with God. We might even think we went looking for God and found Him—in church or the Bible or among Christian friends—when in fact the opposite is true. God in Christ came looking for us, and gently drew us to Himself by these means!

The cultures of the New Testament, and ironically most of the modern world outside of Western culture, presumes that the wider community, especially the nuclear family, is involved in every serious decision, including a change in religious beliefs. Individuals who go their own way are looked upon as odd, misfits, even rebellious. In a sociocentric or homogeneous society, anything an individual accomplishes is believed to be a construct of the wider community and is the result of family influence and empowerment. "Believe in the Lord Jesus," Paul declared to the jailor in Philippi, "and you will be saved, you and your household" (Acts 16:31). Paul said the same to Lydia a short time earlier when, on her confession of faith, Paul baptized her and her entire household (see Acts 16:14–15).

Donald McGavran observed this sociological connectedness during his missionary work in India. Individuals were reticent about becoming a Christian, not for theological reasons, but because "to them becoming a Christian means 'joining another people.' They refuse Christ not for religious reasons, not because they love their sins, but precisely because they love their brethren."[4] Western missionaries working in such community-conscious cultures had to learn that most conversions were "multi-individual mutually interdependent" decisions that happened after group discussions with consent from a recognized community or family authority.[5] Yet, even in such scenarios, every individual perceives the decision as deeply personal.

A retired Bible translator I know tells the story about working with a remote tribe in Asia. For years, he labored with his native coworker to commit their oral language into a written form and then translate God's Word into this new written language. One day, after they had worked for months through the life of Christ, his coworker stopped and stared. "Is there something wrong?" the missionary translator asked his friend. After a long pause the native man asked, "Did your father know about God's carvings?" He used the word "carvings" because the language had no other way to describe written language. "Yes, he did," the missionary replied. After another long pause, the coworker asked, "Did your father's father know about God's carvings?" Again, the missionary replied, "Yes, he did." Another long pause followed. "Did your father's father's father know about God's carvings?" Now, understanding the real question that was on his coworker's mind, he answered one final time. "Yes, my father's father's father knew about God's carvings."

For a person from Western culture, a conversation like this might never happen. The most pressing question for the native man—"Why did it take you so long to bring us this message?"—was encased in the language of his culture's family and community paradigm. Such a paradigm is steadily being lost in Western secular culture.

Why is this important for us? First, we must recognize that

perseverance is harder when we do it on our own. From the first days of creation to the final events of history, God has wired humans for community. Sadly, Western culture is becoming less and less supportive of the values, principles, and behaviors that nurture healthy bonds between people, especially the nuclear family. One of our greatest achievements in life—one that brings the most fulfillment, personal reward, enduring happiness, and empowering source for perseverance in difficulty —is found in this ancient biblical institution. For a single person, the same connections are experienced with Christian friends, a Bible- and Christ-centered church community, and healthy families of origin. Western culture makes it harder to find these things, but they can be found! Christians who have experienced close relationships defend them passionately. Why? Because we have discovered that in Christian family and in the body of Christ, life is rich, meaningful, and safe. Christians experience joyful community in worship and learning, in service, and in sharing life together. Ben Sasse says this about the nuclear family:

> Marriage offers the opportunity to experience genuine, deep friendship. But that takes work. So much love, sweat, and tears go into building a family. You're constantly learning what it means to "die to self." But it's so much better than any two-dimensional counterfeit.[6]

Healthy relationships require work! They take courage, endurance, and an abundance of patience and virtue. They are the grittiest work a human being can do. This is the Mount

Everest of human achievement. It is the one thing in life that makes us wealthier, happier, and more content than anyone else. When we are committed to and have committed people around us, life bursts with possibilities because in these primary relationships, our social needs *are finally met.* The holes in our souls, the ones God designed to be met by other people, are filled and we no longer struggle to fill them. Healthy families grow together, inspired with purpose, empowered to create, motivated to give and serve, and happy to walk beside others on the journey.

Sadly, Western secularism is now steadily replacing this great institution of family with the knockoffs of individualism and self-reliance. These inferior copies are bought by millions like an addictive drug that makes big promises and never delivers. It is understandable why our culture is skeptical about marriage and the family. Too many have never experienced these things in a wholesome way. And yet even skeptics long for the connections and intimacy that marriage and family provide. All human greatness builds on and complements this fundamental God-designed human institution.

Christian apologist and author Ravi Zacharias said that the "point of relevance in our time"—that which most resonates with the postmodern generation—is a hunger for love.[7] Christians have experienced the answer to that hunger. We found love and belonging in Jesus Christ. The love of God has flowed into our individual and corporate lives. As we walk with Jesus in faith and obedience, it overflows into all of our relationships—at home, with friends, and in our communities. There is no more effective witness to the redemption power of Jesus Christ than the love of God expressed in Christian family and community. "Your love for one another will prove to the world that you are my disciples" (John 13:35 NLT).

Wherever you are in life right now, whatever difficulty you're going through, whatever has happened to you in the past, God can help you rediscover His purposes for your life. Ask Him to help you. Read the Bible and get into a healthy church. Deal with your sin, look your demons in the eye and conquer them with God's help, mend relational fences where you can, and commit to building healthy relationships with people who can walk with you in life's journey. If you are married, do everything within your power to make your marriage work. If you are divorced or single, seek to make every new relationship the best and healthiest it can be in Jesus Christ. Walk with faith, patience, and caution. Don't let the influences of culture or your own longings rush you into anything. Be a healthy, single Christ-following person, and seek God fervently about your career, your relationships, and His greatest purposes for your life. Plug into God and His plan with His people! Persevere! The rewards at the end of the journey—the knowledge that you have completed God's designed purpose for you, and finished the course He laid out for you to run— are worth your best and most noble efforts. Press through, find your way, lean on God and a few trusted, Jesus-centered friends, and don't ever, ever quit!

Now may the God of peace himself sanctify you completely, and may your whole spirit and soul and body be kept blameless at the coming of our Lord Jesus Christ. He who calls you is faithful; he will surely do it. (1 Thess. 5:23–24)

ACKNOWLEDGMENTS

This book might never have been written if not for a "chance" meeting in Chicago. I was speaking at a conference and afterward spent about an hour standing around fielding questions from a small group of people. One young man lingered at the back. When the crowd began to thin, I turned to him and he said, "My name is Duane Sherman, I work for Moody Publishers, and I'd like to talk to you about publishing your next book." Over coffee and conversation, we settled on perseverance as the theme. I have Duane to thank for walking beside me for nearly a year in the development of *Before You Quit*. His faithful coaching and encouragement kept me going. The Moody editorial team, especially Michelle Sincock, helped me through multiple manuscript iterations to make the final product shine. I am indebted to everyone at Moody for their tireless work to bring this book to print.

My presence at the above-mentioned conference was the result of an affiliation with the Luis Palau Association and Palau's Next Generation Alliance. David Jones, the director of NGA, arranged for me to speak in Chicago where I met Duane Sherman. Later, with his heavy load of responsibilities and a fight with cancer, Luis Palau graciously took the time to write the Foreword. I am indebted to the entire Palau organization and their investment into my life over many years. The opportunities they have offered me and Globe International have been priceless.

The older I get, the more I have come to realize that the person I am today, and the message or voice I might have to offer the world, is the result, not only of my own decisions and walk, but of a growing list of people who have walked with me. My parents and grandparents lived a lifetime of perseverance in front of me. They did it so naturally and with such ease, no other way of living has ever made sense. My wife, Beth, has stood by my side for over four decades. During the development of this book, my fourth, she again patiently gave me the space and support to write. Our four children, dependent in childhood and youth, have become amazing assets, encouragers, and even coaches to me now in adulthood through their professional acumen and maturity. In many ways, their insights into God's heart and His Word are sharper than my own. Our attorney son, Jeremy, busy in the Air Force and with a wife and three children, plowed through an early version of the manuscript and offered much helpful feedback.

Finally, I want to thank the Globe International leadership team, staff, and board of directors for releasing me to take the time I needed to write. Josh Britnell read the manuscript and offered a young person's perspective on how to improve the content and message. Scott Brown led the Globe cheerleading squad in the arduous process of turning a book *idea* into a reality. Words fail to express what the support of the entire Globe Team has meant to me. I thank God every day for the privilege to work with such a quality group of godly people.

They love Jesus, they love God's people, and they are committed to fulfill Christ's Great Commission to the entire world. My prayer is that this book will help complete that most important of all human endeavors.

NOTES

Introduction

1. The Golden Triangle refers to the border regions between Thailand, Burma, and Laos during a time when gold was used by Chinese traders to pay for the opium grown there. In Southeast Asia, the term is synonymous with the opium and heroin trade. https://en.wikipedia.org/wiki/Golden_Triangle_(Southeast_Asia).
2. The full quote, attributed to William Carey, is, "If he give me credit for being a plodder he will describe me justly. Anything beyond that will be too much. I can plod. I can persevere in any definite pursuit. To this I owe everything."
3. Angela Duckworth, *Grit: The Power and Passion of Perseverance* (Scribner: New York, 2016).

Chapter One: The Battle for Perseverance

1. H. B. Irving, *A Book of Remarkable Criminals* (New York: George H. Doran Company, 1918), 36–98.
2. Leonard Ravenhill, *Why Revival Tarries* (Bloomington, MN: Bethany House Publishers, 1987), 33–34.
3. Timothy Keller, *Walking with God through Pain and Suffering* (New York: Penguin Books, 2013), 14.
4. Stephen Ambrose, *Nothing Like It in the World: The Men Who Built the Transcontinental Railroad 1863–1869* (New York: Simon & Schuster, 2001), 117, is quoted in Gordon MacDonald, *A Resilient Life* (Nashville: Nelson Books, 2004), 43.
5. Matthew 16:24; John 16:33; 2 Corinthians 6:3–5; James 1:2–3.

Chapter Two: Difficulty Involves Loss

1. Eugene H. Peterson, *A Long Obedience in the Same Direction* (Downers Grove, IL: InterVarsity Press, 2000), 16.
2. National Vital Statistics Reports, US Department of Health and Human Services, V66-N6, 11-2017.
3. Lewis Mumford, *Technics and Civilization* (Chicago: University of Chicago Press, 1934), 12.
4. Ibid., 14.
5. Ibid., 15.

6. Neil Postman, *Amusing Ourselves to Death* (New York: Penguin Books, 1985), 11 (emphasis added).
7. Carl Sagan, introduction to *A Brief History of Time*, 1st ed., by Stephen Hawking (New York: Bantam Dell, 1988), x.
8. Lysa Terkeurst, *It's Not Supposed to Be This Way* (Nashville: Nelson Books, 2018), xii.
9. Ibid., 45.
10. *Adrift*, directed by Baltasar Kormakur, produced by Huayi Brothers, Lakeshore Entertainment, RVK Studios, STX Entertainment, 2018.
11. Chris Hedges, *What Every Person Should Know about War* (New York: Free Press, 2005), 1.
12. The story of the Cuban Missile Crisis is documented in Michael Dobbs, *One Minute to Midnight: Kennedy, Khrushchev, and Castro on the Brink of Nuclear War* (New York: Alfred A. Knopf, 2008).
13. "Vietnam War U.S. Military Fatal Casualty Statistics," National Archives, last reviewed on April 30, 2019, https://www.archives.gov/research/military/vietnam-war/casualty-statistics.
14. Neil Postman, *Amusing Ourselves to Death: Public Discourse in the Age of Show Business* (New York: Penguin Books, 1986).
15. Ibid., 87 (emphasis added).
16. David Platt, *Follow Me: A Call to Die, A Call to Live* (Carol Stream, IL: Tyndale, 2013), 109.
17. C. S. Lewis, *The Weight of Glory: And Other Addresses* (New York: HarperCollins Publishers, 2001), 26.
18. The story about an encounter with Jesus by a rich, young ruler is found in the gospels of Matthew (19:16–22), Mark (10:17–22), and Luke (18:18–23). Matthew and Mark say he had "great possessions." Luke says he was "extremely rich." Matthew says he was a "young man." Luke calls him a "ruler." The fact that three gospel writers include the encounter and Jesus' response in their narratives indicates something about the importance of this encounter.
19. Andrew Delbanco, *The Real American Dream: A Meditation of Hope* (Cambridge, MA: Harvard University Press,1999), 2–3. Delbanco quotes Alexis de Tocqueville in his book *Democracy in America*, trans. Phillips Bradley (New York: Vintage, 1990), 107.
20. Don E. Eberly, *The Rise of Global Civil Society: Building Communities and Nations from the Bottom Up* (New York: Encounter Books, 2008), 18–19.
21. Ibid., 43. Survey source: Claire Hughes, "Survey Gives Faith-Based Groups High Marks in Hurricane Aid," The Roundtable on Religion and Social Welfare Policy, December 2005.
22. Timothy Keller, "Praying Our Tears" (sermon, Redeemer Presbyterian Church, NY, February 27, 2000), *Gospel in Life* podcast, https://gospelinlife.com/downloads/praying-our-tears/ (emphasis added).

Chapter Three: Everyday Endurance

1. Gordon MacDonald, *A Resilient Life: You Can Move Ahead No Matter What* (Nashville: Nelson Books, 2004), 66.
2. Romans 3:13–18. I suggest the reader studies this text in several translations to get the full impact of Paul's and the Jewish (by his reference of Psalm 14) view on the sinfulness of man.
3. C. S. Lewis, *The Problem of Pain* (1940; repr., New York: HarperCollins Publishers, 1996), 40. In the quote, Lewis references Revelation 4:11 KJV.
4. Mark 7:21–23; Luke 12:15; Rom. 1:29; 7:7–8; 1 Cor. 5:11; 6:10; 2 Cor. 9:5; Eph. 5:5; James 4:1–2.
5. Patrick Spenner and Karen Freeman, "To Keep Your Customers, Keep It Simple," *Harvard Business Review*, May 2012.
6. Sheena S. Iyengar and Mark R. Lepper, "When Choice is Demotivating: Can One Desire Too Much of a Good Thing?," *Journal of Personality and Social Psychology* 79, no. 6 (2000): 1003.
7. Barry Schwartz, "The Tyranny of Choice," *Scientific American* 290, no. 4 (2004): 70–75.
8. Mihaly Csikszentmihalyi, *Creativity: Flow and the Psychology of Discovery and Invention* (New York: HarperCollins Publishers, 1996), 110.
9. John Ortberg, *Soul Keeping: Caring for the Most Important Part of You* (Grand Rapids: Zondervan, 2014), 20.

Chapter Four: Aspirations for Greatness

1. See http://www.ironman.com; Will Gray, "Be an IRONMAN Expert with These Stats on This Month's World Championships," Red Bull, October 1, 2019, https://www.redbull.com/us-en/kona-ironman-stats.
2. Angela Duckworth, *Grit: The Power and Passion of Perseverance* (New York: Scribner, 2016), 39.
3. Malcolm Gladwell, *Outliers: The Story of Success* (Columbus, GA: Little, Brown and Company, 2011), 41.
4. Ibid., 37.
5. Ibid., 39 (emphasis added). The word "much" in bold was italicized by Gladwell in the original text.
6. Duckworth, *Grit*, 54–58.
7. Ibid., 143.
8. Ibid., 147–48.
9. Ibid., 83.
10. Henry Cloud, *The Power of the Other* (New York: HarperCollins Publishers, 2016), 9.
11. Ibid., 2.

Chapter Five: Greatness from God's Perspective

1. A. W. Tozer, *I Talk Back to the Devil: The Fighting Fervor of the Victorious Christian* (1972; repr., Chicago: Moody, 2018), 26.
2. Joey Buran, *Beyond the Dream* movie, produced by AquaFluence and Tight Productions, 2009.
3. Pastor Mike Doyle, www.movementnyc.org.
4. Count Zinzendorf, quoted in Janet and Geoff Benge, *Count Zinzendorf: Firstfruit*, Christian Heroes: Then & Now (Seattle: YWAM Publishing, 2005), 102.
5. Tozer, *I Talk Back to the Devil*, 26 (emphasis added).
6. Angela Duckworth, *Grit: The Power and Passion of Perseverance* (New York: Scribner, 2016), 79.

Chapter Six: Moral Courage

1. John D. Morris, "The Survival of Noah's Ark," Institute for Creation Research, December 28, 2012, https://www.icr.org/article/survival-noahs-ark.
2. John Woodmorappe, *Noah's Ark: A Feasibility Study* (El Cajon, CA: Institute for Creation Research, 1996).
3. Genesis 37–48 recounts the incredible story of Joseph's life from son, to slave, to ruler.
4. Mary Fairchild, "Heroes of Faith in the Book of Hebrews," Learn Religions, updated June 25, 2019, https://www.learnreligions.com/hebrews-chapter-11-heroes-of-faith-700176.
5. Friedrich Wilhelm Nietzsche, quoted by Harold S. Kushner, foreword to Viktor Frankl, *Man's Search for Meaning* (New York: Simon & Schuster, New York, 1984), ix. Quote originally appeared in Nietzsche's *Twilight of the Idols*.
6. John Piper, *Let the Nations Be Glad: The Supremacy of God in Missions*, 3rd ed. (Grand Rapids: Baker Academic, 2010), 50.
7. Steve Hawthorne, *Perspectives Reader*, 4th ed. (Pasadena, CA: William Carey Library, 2009), 49.
8. The term *sovereignty* encompasses God's omnipotence (all power), omniscience (all knowledge), omnipresence (all presence), His eternal nature, etc.
9. Hawthorne, *Perspectives Reader*, 49.
10. www.perspectives.org. The "Perspectives on the World Christian Movement" course is a fifteen-week course conceived and formed by Dr. Ralph Winter in 1973. Since then, "Perspectives" has been studied by hundreds of thousands of people all over the United States and the world. It is offered at certificate, undergraduate, and graduate levels.
11. This brief summary of Adoniram Judson's life story is taken from

Janet and Geoff Benge, *Adoniram Judson: Bound for Burma* (Seattle: YWAM Publishing, 2000).
12. Piper, *Let the Nations Be Glad*, 60–61.

Chapter Seven: Perseverance and God's Consummate Purposes

1. A. W. Tozer, *Jesus Is Victor: A Fresh Perspective on the Book of Revelation* (Camp Hill, PA: WingSpread Publishers, 2010), 10–11.
2. Acts 2:14–17; 1 Peter 4:7; Rev. 1:1–3 are a few references to New Testament writers who believed the end of the age was near. They were not wrong on this point. Since the day of Pentecost in Acts 2, we are living in the final age, the last days. We do not know the day nor the hour, but as people of the new covenant, we live with the joyful anticipation of the glorious return of Jesus.
3. Eugene H. Peterson, *A Long Obedience in the Same Direction: Discipleship in an Instant Society* (Downers Grove, IL: InterVarsity Press, 2000), 76.
4. Eric Metaxas, *Bonhoeffer: Pastor, Martyr, Prophet, Spy* (Nashville: Thomas Nelson, 2010), 381 (emphasis added).
5. Ibid., 383.
6. Ibid., 528.
7. For a longer treatment of Jesus' "endure to the end" teaching, refer to Matthew 10:16–22, where Jesus first commissions His apostles.
8. David Platt, *Follow Me: A Call to Die, A Call to Live* (Carol Stream, IL: Tyndale, 2013), 87.
9. C. S. Lewis, *The Problem of Pain* (New York: HarperCollins Publishers, 1996), 124–25. C. S. Lewis quotes Von Hugel in his *Essays and Addresses*, 1st series, "What Do We Mean by Heaven and Hell?"

Chapter Eight: Self-Care: Thriving in Difficulty

1. Marvin Olasky, "Facing Waves," *WORLD*, August 16, 2018, https://world.wng.org/2018/08/facing_waves.
2. William Evans, *The Great Doctrines of the Bible* (Chicago: Moody, 1974), 5.
3. Gordon MacDonald, *A Resilient Life: You Can Move Ahead No Matter What* (Nashville: Nelson Books, 2004), 170.
4. Robert H. Shmerling, "Right Brain/Left Brain, Right?," Harvard Health Publishing, posted August 25, 2017, updated November 8, 2019, https://www.health.harvard.edu/blog/right-brainleft-brain-right-2017082512222. Schmerling references a peer-reviewed research article entitled "An Evaluation of the Left-Brain vs. Right-Brain Hypothesis with Resting State Functional Connectivity Magnetic Resonance Imaging," published on August 14, 2013, by Jared A. Nielson,

Brandon A. Zielinski, Michael A. Ferguson, Janet E. Lainhart, and Jeffrey S. Anderson. The article is available at https://journals.plos.org/plosone/article?id=10.1371/journal.pone.0071275.

5. Eugene H. Peterson, *A Long Obedience in the Same Direction: Discipleship in an Instant Society* (Downers Grove, IL: InterVarsity Press, 2000), 54.

6. Paul Carter, "Dashing the Little Ones Against the Rock—Does This Verse Really Belong in Scripture?," The Gospel Coalition, July 5, 2017, https://ca.thegospelcoalition.org/columns/ad-fontes/dashing-little-ones-rock-verse-really-belong-scripture/.

7. Ibid.

8. Ibid.

9. Andrea Palpant Dilley, *Faith and Flat Tires*, quoted in Timothy Keller, *Walking with God through Pain and Suffering*, 106.

10. Ibid., 106.

11. Mihaly Csikszentmihalyi, *Creativity: Flow and the Psychology of Discovery and Invention* (New York: HarperCollins Publishers, 1996), 8. Csikszentmihalyi distinguishes between "Creativity" as a function of professionals and "creativity" as an expression of all people for distraction and soul health.

12. The Genesis 1–2 account of creation includes the repeated commentary by God that "He saw and it was good."

13. Philip Graham Ryken, *Written in Stone: The Ten Commandments and Today's Moral Crisis* (Wheaton, IL: Crossway, 2003), 104.

14. Richard Winter, *Still Bored in a Culture of Entertainment: Rediscovering Passion & Wonder* (Downers Grove, IL: InterVarsity Press, 2002), 33.

15. Ibid., 73. Winter quotes William F. May, *A Catalogue of Sins: A Contemporary Examination of Christian Conscience* (New York: Holt, Rinehart & Winston, 1967), 195–96 (emphasis added).

Chapter Nine: Perseverance as a Lifestyle

1. Blake Snyder, *Save the Cat: The Last Book on Screenwriting You'll Ever Need* (Studio City, CA: Michael Wise Productions, 2005), xv.

2. *Rocky Balboa*, written/directed by Sylvester Stallone, Metro-Goldwyn-Mayer, Columbia Pictures, 2006.

3. Donald Miller, *A Million Miles in a Thousand Years* (Nashville: Thomas Nelson, 2011).

4. Timothy Keller, "Justice," Gospel in Life Sermons Podcast, February 19, 2010.

5. Gordon MacDonald, *A Resilient Life: You Can Move Ahead No Matter What* (Nashville: Nelson Books, 2004), 16.

6. Genesis 3 recounts the "fall" of humankind into sin by disobedience to God's command. That Adam and Eve were tempted by the serpent

does not absolve them of responsibility. Their attempt to shift responsibility is the story of fallen humanity ever since. Repentance is the first step in healing, because it takes responsibility. In His grace, God foretold His plan of redemption through Jesus Christ (Gen. 3:14–15).

7. The story about an encounter with Jesus by a rich young ruler is found in Matthew 19:16–22, Mark 10:17–22, and Luke 18:18–23.
8. Timothy Keller, *Walking with God through Pain and Suffering* (New York: Penguin Books, 2016), 77.
9. Caroline Alexander, *The Endurance: Shackleton's Legendary Antarctic Expedition* (New York: Alfred A. Knopf, 2001), from the cover.
10. Ibid., 5.
11. Ibid.
12. Ibid., 5–6 (emphasis added).

Epilogue

1. Ben Sasse, *Them: Why We Hate Each Other* (New York: St. Martin's Press, 2018), 23.
2. Ibid., 3.
3. Ibid., 206.
4. Donald A. McGavran, *Understanding Church Growth*, Fully Revised (Grand Rapids: William B. Eerdmans Publishing Company, 1980), 214.
5. Ibid., 339–40.
6. Sasse, *Them*, 211.
7. Ravi Zacharias, "The Touch of Truth," in *Telling the Truth: Evangelizing Postmoderns*, ed. D. A. Carson (Grand Rapids: Zondervan, 2000), 38.